MOUNTAIN BIKING IN THE PEAK DISTRICT

Paul Wake & Paul Woodrow

Published by Sigma Leisure – an imprint of
Sigma Press, 1 South Oak Lane, Wilmslow, Cheshire SK9 6AR, England.

British Library Cataloguing in Publication Data
A CIP record for this book is available from the British Library.

ISBN: 1-85058-704-3

Typesetting and Design by: Sigma Press, Wilmslow, Cheshire.

Printed by: MFP Design & Print

Cover Photograph: Peak Forest from Eldon Hill
(Tim Woodcock)

Photographs: the authors and John Woodrow

Cartoons: Brian Sage

Maps: Michael Gilbert

DISCLAIMER

THANKS!

Thanks from both of us go out to Andrew for getting the whole thing started, the Wakes for putting up with us most weekends and Mr Woodrow for the photos. Also, in no particular order, a big shout out to Richard @ Specialized, Shelley @ Continental, Richard @ Madison, Amanda @ Endura, Leslie @ Polaris, Sue @ Berghaus, Lillian @ Terra Nova, Paul @ Michelin, everyone at Harry Hall in Manchester and Nick @ KG Bikes in Glossop.

Contents

LOCATION MAP

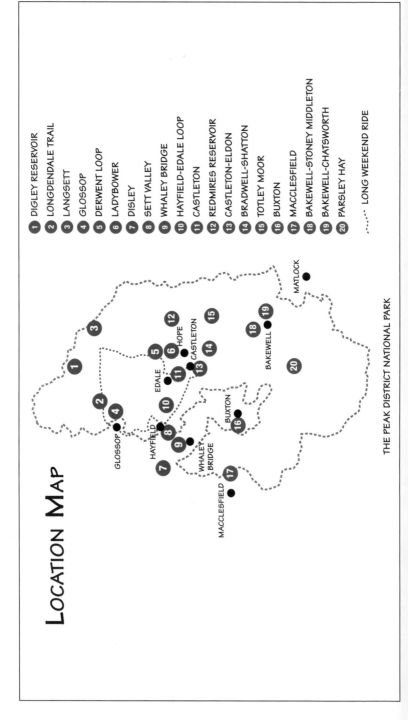

1. DIGLEY RESERVOIR
2. LONGDENDALE TRAIL
3. LANGSETT
4. GLOSSOP
5. DERWENT LOOP
6. LADYBOWER
7. DISLEY
8. SETT VALLEY
9. WHALEY BRIDGE
10. HAYFIELD-EDALE LOOP
11. CASTLETON
12. REDMIRES RESERVOIR
13. CASTLETON-ELDON
14. BRADWELL-SHATTON
15. TOTLEY MOOR
16. BUXTON
17. MACCLESFIELD
18. BAKEWELL-STONEY MIDDLETON
19. BAKEWELL-CHATSWORTH
20. PARSLEY HAY

······ LONG WEEKEND RIDE

THE PEAK DISTRICT NATIONAL PARK

INTRODUCTION

The routes contained in this book are the sort of rides that we enjoy ourselves. This means that a 'good' ride will include at least one fast-and-adrenaline-pumping downhill stretch that can be approached with that unique mix of trepidation, care and speed. In order to get to the top of these descents we try to keep our climbing on smoother, swifter, tracks. That said, there are some classic ascents in here including Lantern Pike, Roych Clough and the infamous Jacob's Ladder. With a few notable exceptions, we've aimed for a ride length of around two to three hours – partly to make it easy to fit a ride or two in at some time during the week and partly because this is the length of time that our stamina levels allow us to happily blast around for. Oh, and all our rides are circuits because we reckon that it's important to be able to get back to your car/railway station. The sheer variety of trails in the Peak Park means that these rides are all quite different. We've given each route gradings and there should be something to appeal to just about everyone from the novice to the expert.

The scenery of the Peak District can be rugged and wind swept, often beautiful, and in our opinion all of these rides take in the best of the great outdoors, but feel free to choose your own sites of beauty. Here and there, we've also mentioned some of the more interesting tourist attractions like Chatsworth House and the Disley Ostriches, but mainly this is a mountain biking guide.

Most of all though, the thing that we enjoy is the company of our mates. Someone to share the excitement with on reaching the bottom of a new, almost vertical, hill. We ride to enjoy ourselves. We hope you will.

Mountain Biking in the Peak District

The Peak District is undoubtedly one of the Britain's finest areas for mountain biking. Packed into its 542 square miles are stacks of great trails, from the bleak expanse of the Dark Peak in the north, where dusky millstone surfaces from vast peat moors, to the more rolling terrain of the White Peak in the south, so called for its characteristic pale limestone dales. Somewhat perversely, considering its name, the 'Peak' district lacks any serious mountains; that said, it is rarely flat – when cycling here, you'll either be climbing out of deep valleys or hurtling down into one. It's perfect.

Getting there

Luckily for us Mountain Bikers, the Peak District is one of the most accessible of our national parks with around half of the population living within a two-hour drive of its centre. Each of the routes in this guide starts from one of the Peak's many small towns – some are accessible by train, some aren't. Here are our top travel tips to help you get to the Peak:

Live there:
– it's an attitude.

Use the Trains:
– from Manchester for stations to Buxton. Trains to Hope (and Edale etc) from Sheffield/Manchester and intermediate stations.

Go by car:
From Down South: Take the M1 up to Sheffield (Junction 30) then take the A621, A619, A6. You're looking for signs to places like Buxton and Bakewell.
From the North West: You shouldn't need directions: get the A537, A54 route via Macclesfield, or the A6 through Stockport, Hazel Grove, and up to Chapel-en-le-Frith.
From Up North: Take the M6 to Preston (Junction 30), M61 all the way, the M63 to the Stockport Pyramid (Junction 12). Then hop onto the A6 through Hazel Grove etc. Easy.

Equipment

We both ride full-suspension bikes which seem to be the choice of almost all riders here in the Peak. The move to full suspension bikes has opened up bigger tougher terrain and our rides tend to reflect this; seeking out the best trails and the biggest thrills. One thing we'd really recommend is investing in a pair of quality tyres. Our current favourites come from the tyre kings Michelin and Continental. Michelin's *Wildgrippers* – the now classic green tyres – offer excellent traction on softer ground and shed mud admirably in wet conditions, over the last couple of years these tyres have proved themselves time and again on the Peak's testing terrain. Continental are still producing their excellent *cross country* tyres which make a perfect choice for the rear offering a well-balanced compromise between traction and speed. Another worthwhile investment is a set of quality off-road lights. We've been running a set of VistaLites over the winter months and they've been superb – night riding not only lets you extend your riding time but it forces you to ride a lot more precisely. Oh – and best of all – it's highly entertaining.

The Trusty Steed: lightweight full-suspension bikes are well-suited to the Peak's rocky trails

Software

If you're planning to cycle for more than three months of the year then it pays to get hold of the best outdoor clothing that you can afford. Here's a selection of the stuff that we've used over the last year...

Porelle Drys – lovely warm waterproof socks. Feel a bit funny and cost plenty but do the job better than anything else. Keep those extremities warm...

Endura Dakota Jacket – The Dakota jacket uses Breath, 'a soft and tactile polyester face fabric with a modified poly-urethane coating on the inside.' In real terms this means that it is excellent at keeping you warm and dry, keeping out both wind and rain. The over-the-head design has long side zips which gives it a good fit and as much ventilation as you want - it practically turns into a cape. The zips are well-placed and have internal storm flaps which haven't let any water through even in particularly unpleasant winter. What's more the Dakota even looks good.

Polaris Stormlight Jacket – The Stormlight is excellently de-signed, with Scotchlight reflective patches, and an inner webbed layer which takes moisture (sweat) away from the rider's body. The seams are taped and are placed on the un-derside and back of the jacket, to ensure that rain cannot be driven through them. Other features include a padded col-lar for comfort and wind protection and elasticated draw-strings at the bottom of the coat for extra protection. If you add to this already formidable mixture a sexy, detachable, peaked hood, you have a coat that keeps you dry as a bone in the most miserable of weather conditions. Excellent.

Endura Thermal Cycling Tights – If you want to keep cycling between October and March, then thermal tights are essen-tial. Endura's tights are warm and hard-wearing. They repel rain and wick sweat away from the rider's legs – clever. They are made in a bib style and have chunky ankle zips, which al-low them to be put on with ease. The ankles are gripped to ensure that puddles won't wet your legs. This book could not have been completed without these tights!

Trail Kit

This is the stuff that you're going to take with you on the ride. What you take has to strike a balance between function and weight. Carrying loads of stuff is a pain but then so is being stuck with a broken bike in the rain miles from shelter. There are two ways to go – individual tools or a multi-tool. Whichever you choose you should include: Allen keys/screwdriver set, a chain tool, a puncture repair kit, a pump and at least one inner tube. Invest in some good tools and they'll repay you tenfold, for guaranteed quality we'd go for these tools every time. In fact there's no 'every time' about it – you buy these tools once and they last pretty much forever. Depending on the type of ride and the time of year you might want to also think about taking along a whistle, compass, survival bag and a mobile phone.

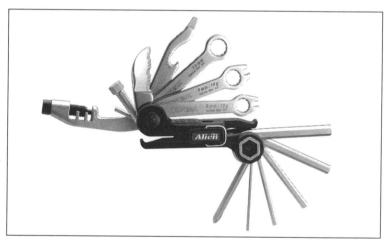

'The Alien' multi-tool is a viable alternative to carrying individual tools

Navigation

A fair ability to map read has been assumed in the production of this guide. The routes and maps are intended to be used in conjunction with the relevant Ordnance Survey map, and a compass wouldn't go amiss on some of the higher level routes (**note:** a compass will give false readings if held near a steel bike frame or handlebars). If you need to brush up on your map reading, take a look at Eric Langmuir's *Mountaincraft and Leadership* which contains an excellent, if lengthy, discussion of the art of map reading.

Route Descriptions

Each route starts with a brief introduction to give an idea of the ride and to highlight any particularly good or otherwise noteworthy sections. The route descriptions have been written to be as clear and concise as possible – we've split the description up at what should be pretty logical points so that each section has quite a clear start and finish point. These checkpoints have been marked with a corresponding letter on the accompanying sketch maps. The trail conditions are described: sections of singletrack (narrow paths) are mentioned, as are sections of hardpack (smooth 'all-weather' tracks) and any rocky tracks. For those of you who have cycle computers we've included a running total of the distance covered (**DISTANCE SO FAR**, or **DSF**) at the end of each section. These were taken from two different cycle computers and any minor differences were averaged out to compensate for riding style; we also reset at each checkpoint to avoid any cumulative errors.

Route Gradings

The route descriptions all contain two gradings: one for fitness and the other for technical ability. Rides with a grading of either one or two (indicated by filled-in discs: ● or ●●) in each category are quite gentle routes and should be suitable for novice riders. Grading three might be regarded as the first true off-road routes and take the rider that little bit further and can contain some pretty challenging terrain, but nothing too extreme. Rides of grading four are getting tougher with climbs and descents that will probably make novice riders get off and walk. Grade five is aimed at the experienced rider with some climbs, like Jacob's Ladder, that almost no one will get up, and some descents that really do warrant at least front suspension. This said, the gradings are all relative to one another and to our own levels of skill and fitness, so work out where you fit in and take it from there.

Sketch Maps

We have included detailed sketch maps for each route, the scale of these maps is given in each instance. The check-points marked on the maps correspond to those in the text for easy cross-referencing. In addition to the sketch maps included in this book, we recommend the use of one of the following large-scale maps:

Ordnance Survey
Outdoor Leisure Map 1, *Dark Peak* (1:25,000)
Outdoor Leisure Map 24, *White Peak* (1:25,000)

Harveys' Maps
Superwalker Map *Dark Peak North* (1:25,000)
Superwalker Map *Dark Peak South* (1:25,000)

Laminated maps are an excellent idea and can be obtained from good map stockists or direct from Chartech on (01433) 621779.

Key to Sketch Maps

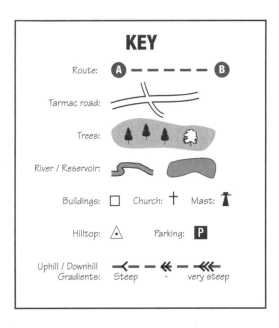

Route One
DIGLEY RESERVOIR

Total Distance: 7.25 miles (11.67 km)

Off-road: 4.66 miles (7.50 km) (64%)

Time taken: 1½ hours

OS Map: Outdoor Leisure 1, *Dark Peak*

Start: Digley Reservoir car park (GR SE109068)

Rail Access: Not really.

Difficulty Ratings

Technical: ●●●○○

Fitness: ●●●○○ (the only real challenge is the climb from Royd Farm to the A635)

As the British Tourist Board might say, this is the type of ride that the weather can't spoil, and we should know because we've ridden it when it's been nasty. Much of the climbing is kept on tarmac, the chief exception to this being the long climb up Royd Farm/Magdalen Road, which I always think of as a push. The backdrop at this point is of grey hills and rugged moorlands – the Peak District at its best. The soil drainage around here must be of a very high standard, as the bridleways never seem to get too muddy whilst the descent along Nether Lane reminds you why it's good to be out on your bike whatever the weather . . . for FUN!

The Route

A   **Digley Reservoir car park:** Turn left out of the car park and cycle across the reservoir's dam. Turn left at the end of the road and ride uphill staying on Green Gate Road until you reach a cross roads with the A635 opposite the 'Ford Inn'.
DISTANCE SO FAR (DSF): 1.22 miles (1.96 km).

B   **Ford Inn/A635:** Turn left onto the A635 until you see a signposted bridleway on the right. It's a pretty obvious track but look out for the 'Huntsman' pub sign just next to the track.
DSF: 1.48 miles (2.38 km).

C   **Harden Hill Road:** Head uphill on the well-surfaced farm track (Harden Hill Road), just beyond a farmhouse the track deteriorates and heads off downhill between two stone walls. Continue along to the end of this rutted bridleway as it heads downwards, to meet the road at Royd Bridge.
DSF: 2.60 miles (4.18 km).

D   **Royd Bridge:** Turn left and head uphill for a steep tarmac climb. The road reaches a junction with a bridleway heading off and upwards to the left (effectively this is straight on), stay with the road and follow it round sharply to the right.
DSF: 2.98 miles (4.80 km).

E   **Royd Farm/Magdalen Road:** Follow the road past Royd Farm. The track soon deteriorates and becomes a faint grass path climbing gently, but persistently, around the side of Round Hill. Keep the stone wall to your left and you won't go wrong. Continue upwards for a little over a mile until you meet a gate. Go through the gate and descend to meet the A635.
DSF: 4.17 miles (6.71 km).

F   **A635/Springs Road:** Turn right onto the A635 and almost immediately drop down left onto the obvious bridleway. Head gently downhill along this semi-paved track until you reach a gate/stile that blocks your way straight on. The bridleway, now Nether Lane, heads off sharp left.
DSF: 4.87 miles (7.84 km).

G   **Nether Lane:** Follow the road around to the left for a fast descent on the wide hardpack track. After the initial descent, the track undulates gently until it meets a T-junction with Acres lane.
DSF: 6.62 miles (10.65 km).

H   **Acres Lane:** Turn right onto tarmac and cycle down the road. Turn right at the crossroads with Green Gate Road and ride down the road, across the dam to arrive back at the car park.
TOTAL DISTANCE: 7.25 miles (11.67 km).

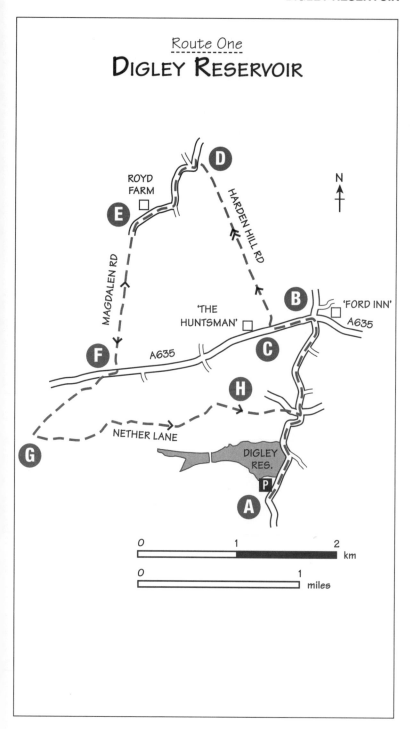

Route Two

LONGDENDALE TRAIL

Total Distance: 13.13 miles (21.22 km) *or* 17.24 miles (27.74 km)
Off-road: 13.13 miles (21.22 km) (100%) *or* 15.00 miles (24.14 km) (87%)
Time taken: 1½ – 2 hours
OS Map: Outdoor Leisure 1, Dark Peak
Start: Padfield (GR SK026962)
Rail Access: Padfield Station is about one hundred metres from the start.

Difficulty Ratings

Technical: ●○○○○
(You've got to be able to ride a bike . . .)

or　　　　●●○○○

Fitness:　●○○○○
(Turn round when you're getting tired)

or　　　　●●○○○

This is an out-and-back ride along the Longdendale trail, which used to be a railway. The whole ride is pretty flat and the track is smooth hardpack all the way. But be warned: the trail is popular, and for good reason, with families and some of the younger riders are less than sure which side of the trail to ride . . . we saw this cause more than one wipe-out on our ride. The best bit of this ride is the scenery: the views over Torside and Woodhead reservoirs are truly stunning.

We've included a supplement to the ride that adds in a bit of slightly rougher terrain, an easy climb leads up to a fairly long and enjoyable down from the top of Pikenaze Hill. The downside of this last section is that it is reached by two brief road sections on the very busy A628 which are not exactly child-friendly.

The Route

A **Padfield:** The ride starts from the car park (space for around 16 cars) at the Padfield end of the Longdendale trail. Join the trail and head NE. Continue along the hardpack trail with the reservoir on your left until the trail meets the B6105.
DISTANCE SO FAR (DSF): 2.58 miles (4.15 km).

B **B6105:** Cross the road and pick up the trail on the other side. Continue along the trail until you reach a sign directing you to the information centre down on your left. If you fancy refreshment, it's a quick drop down to the National Park information centre where there's a car park, toilets, and usually an ice cream van (it's 0.12 miles); otherwise, continue along the trail until you reach the dam at Woodhead Reservoir.
DSF: 5.55 miles (8.93 km).

C **Woodhead Reservoir:** Continue along the trail with Woodhead Reservoir on your left until you reach an old station and blocked-up tunnel.
DSF: 6.59 miles (10.61 km).

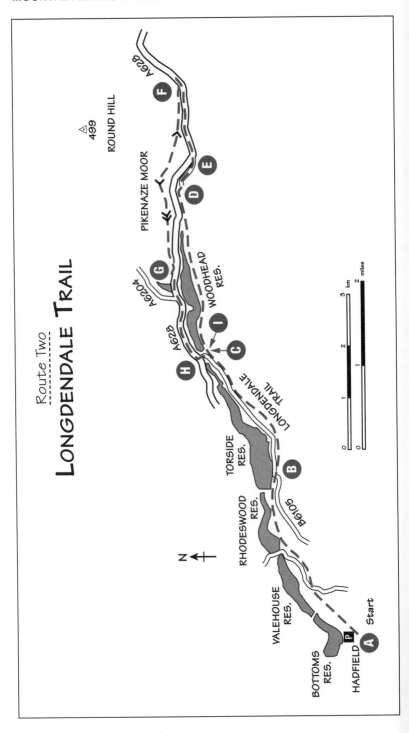

Route Two

LONGDENDALE TRAIL

D **Woodhead Tunnels:** This is the time to turn around unless you feel like something a little more challenging. Assuming you opt to turn around, simply retrace the route until you find yourself back in Padfield.
TOTAL DISTANCE #1: 13.18 miles (21.22 km).

The Extra Section

E **Woodhead Tunnels:** Continue through the old station and climb up the tarmac road until you meet the A628.
DSF: 6.85 miles (11.02 km).

F **A628:** Turn right onto the very busy A628 and climb for just over a mile until you meet a bridleway signposted for the Longdendale Trail on your left, heading back the way you have just come.
DSF: 7.93 miles (12.76 km).

G **Longside End:** Turn left onto the bridleway which is a fairly wide semi-cobbled road climbing gently up Longside, ending with a long off-road descent down Pikenaze Hill. At the bottom of the descent, head through the five-barred gate and roll down a short stretch of tarmac to meet the A628.
DSF: 10.53 miles (16.95 km).

H **A628:** Turn right onto the A628, cross Woodhead bridge and ride along until you reach the left turn across Woodhead Reservoir, signposted 'Glossop – B6105'.
DSF: 11.46 miles (18.44 km).

I **Woodhead Dam:** Ride across the dam to rejoin the Longdendale trail.
DSF: 11.69 miles (18.81 km).

J **Longdendale Trail:** You'll know where you are now. Join the trail and head right (SW) until you reach the car park in Padfield.
TOTAL DISTANCE #2: 17.24 miles (27.74 km).

Route Three
LANGSETT

Total Distance: 6.13 miles (9.87 km)

Off-road: 4.49 miles (7.23 km) (73%)

Time taken: 2 hours

OS Map: Outdoor Leisure 1, *Dark Peak*

Start: Langsett Barn car park (GR SE211005)

Rail Access: The nearest station is in Penistone.

Difficulty Ratings

Technical: ●●●○○

Fitness: ●●●○○ (if the weather is not fine, this becomes a very challenging ride)

This route is short, fast and furious, with some sections being technical enough to challenge all but the gnarliest of riders. There is a marvellous, top-notch, lengthy descent along Mickleden Edge, and of course the usual boggy moor sections which, on this occasion, are found close to North America Farm. Be warned, should the weather turn nasty, the area around Mickleden Edge is very exposed and you will need your most thermal of winter garments. Added to this, there are no shops once you leave Langsett – so take drinks and Snickers along with you.

The Route

A **Langsett Barn car park:** Turn right out of the car park onto the busy A616. Roll down the hill through Langsett, looking out for a right turn just after the 'Wagon and Horses' pub onto Midhope Cliff Lane. Turn right onto this minor road and follow it round to the right through Upper Midhope. Just through Upper Midhope the road takes a sharp left turn at which point you should see the start of Thickwoods Lane heading roughly straight on.
DISTANCE SO FAR (DSF): 1.10 miles (1.77 km).

B **Thickwoods Lane:** Follow Thickwoods Lane through the trees, through two gates and then upward and out along the side of the wood until you reach the ruins of North America Farm.
DSF: 1.96 miles (3.15 km).

C **North America Farm Ruins:** Turn left (SW) just before the ruins (don't go through the gate into the ruins) and ride in a roughly south-westerly direction up the moor. Initially keeping the wall on your right, follow this rocky, often boggy, path up until you meet Mickleden Edge.
DSF: 2.97 miles (4.78 km).

D   **Mickleden Edge:** Turn right onto Mickleden Edge. Follow the path, which is rocky at the top and increasingly smooth (if it's not too wet) as it loses height until you arrive at Brookhouse Bridge. Just before the bridge, it gets a bit steeper and more technical.
DSF: 4.45 miles (7.93 km).

Heading down to Brookhouse

E   **Brookhouse Bridge:** Cross the bridge and climb out of the valley into the trees. At the top of the first climb, take the right fork and head east on the smooth forest road following it around to the right until you emerge on the A616.
DSF: 4.93 miles (8.21 km).

F   **A616:** Turn right onto the concessionary bridleway that runs parallel with the A616 until it ends a couple of hundred metres further down the road. Look out for the bridleway on the opposite side of the road and cross the A616 to ride up it.
DSF: 5.10 miles (9.03 km).

G   **Fulshaw Hill:** Cycle up the bridleway which is a wide and often muddy farm track sandwiched between two stone walls which will drop you down to meet a minor road called Gilbert Hill. Turn right.
DSF: 5.61 miles (9.03 km).

H   **Gilbert Hill:** Roll down Gilbert Hill until it meets the A616. Turn right and cycle on a short way until you reach the car park on your left.
TOTAL DISTANCE: 6.13 miles (9.87 km).

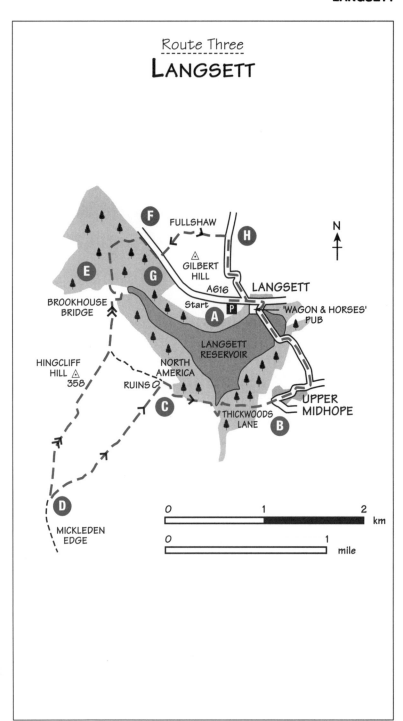

Route Three
LANGSETT

Route Four
GLOSSOP SNAKE

Total Distance: 10.09 miles (16.24 km)
Off-road: 3.95 miles (6.36 km) (39%)
Time taken: 2 hours
OS Map: Outdoor Leisure 1, *Dark Peak*
Start: Glossop Station car park (GR SK035942)
Rail Access: Glossop Station.

Difficulty Ratings
Technical: ●●●○○
Fitness: ●●●○○

Do you have a couple of hours free on a Sunday afternoon? You could do a lot worse than try this ride. This one's a simple out-and-back ride that takes in the Snake Pass which, you'll be interested to know, wasn't named after the twisty nature of its 'snaking path' but rather because of the snake on the crest of the Cavendish family (the Dukes of Devonshire). Remember that it is jolly high at the top of the Snake Pass, and therefore gets pretty cold – so wrap up warm. As ever, the up is on road and the down is off-road. Be careful, the paths are narrow, the drops are long and the landings rocky. Don't be fooled by the term 'Roman Road' used by the OS people as a euphemism for the rocky track that you ride down, although there is one very fast swoopy downhill right at the end. Enjoy.

The Route

A   **Glossop Station car park:** Turn right out of the car park, and turn left at the traffic lights, onto the A57. This road leads to the Snake Pass. Follow it uphill for 4.80 miles. You pass one turn off for the bridleway, and start to descend for the last half mile. Turn left on Doctor's Gate at the lay-by on the left.
DISTANCE SO FAR (DSF): 4.80 miles (7.72 km).

B   **Doctor's Gate:** Follow the track initially away from the road. Cross the ford, and follow the paving flag track. Go straight across at the four way crossroads, and follow the very rough broken track/Roman Road. Initially, keep the river on your right. After three miles, and a couple of crossings of the river, you hit a smooth fast downhill. Go through a gate at the bottom and take the right-hand bridge. Don't take the left, which leads to a farm.
DSF: 8.75 miles (14.08 km).

A Roman does his own stunts!

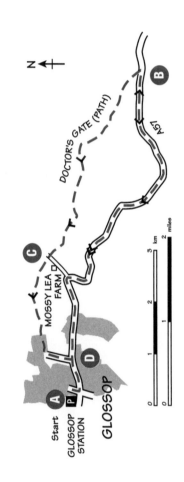

Route Four
GLOSSOP SNAKE

C   **Sheply Street:** After another mile, and a second gate, the track turns into Sheply Street. Follow this for 0.20 miles and turn left at the T-junction, past the Post Office. Follow this road for 0.33 miles to a second T-junction. Turn right, back onto the A57.
DSF: 9.28 miles (14.93 km).

D   **A57:** Roll down the hill for half a mile, until you reach the four way junction near the railway station. Turn right, you're home.
TOTAL DISTANCE: 10.09 miles (16.24 km).

Route Five

DERWENT LOOP

Total Distance: 10.73 miles (17.27 km)
Off-road: 5.33 miles (8.58 km) (50%)
Time taken: 1½ hours
OS Map: Outdoor Leisure Map 1, *Dark Peak*
Start: Fairholmes Visitors Centre (GR SK173893)
Rail Access: Hope station is the nearest option.

Difficulty Ratings

Technical: ●○○○○
Fitness: ●●○○○

This relatively easy ride takes in one of the Peak's most beautiful areas – the landscape around Derwent reservoir. It is almost entirely flat and keeps to nice smooth off-road tracks with stunning views and a couple of enticing picnic spots. Starting out from the well-equipped Visitor Centre which has ample parking, toilets, information centre, bike hire, an excellent hot food shack. From here, the ride sets out along the side of the reservoir on a quiet, almost traffic-free, road before heading off-road into the trees. The midpoint of the ride is marked by a 17th-century stone bridge, which makes a great stop-off point for a picnic. The rest is all on fairly smooth and well-drained hardpack which takes you back around the far side of the reservoirs to the base of the magnificent Derwent dam where, as everyone will tell you, the Dambusters practised with their prototype bouncing bombs. If you resisted the temptation to picnic at the bridge then this place is ideal with plenty of space to chuck around that Frisbee you brought along.

The Route

BEWARE LOW-FLYING FRISBEES

A   **Fairholmes Visitor Centre**: Turn right (N) out of the car park and cycle straight across the roundabout through the gate barring motorised traffic. Ride along this quiet tarmacked road keeping the reservoirs, first the Derwent and later the Howden on your right. Eventually you will arrive at the road's end, marked by a mini-roundabout across which you will see a gate leading off-road.
DISTANCE SO FAR (DSF): 4.95 miles (7.97 km).

B   **Upper Wood:** Head through the gate onto a gently undulating hardpack track leading you through the trees. Ford the shallow stream, or cross the stepping stones, and continue along the track until it dips down out of the trees to meet a 17th-century stone bridge that takes you across the river Derwent.
DSF: 5.82 miles (9.37 km).

C **Stone Bridge:** Cross the bridge and once across head left, following the signpost that directs you to the bridleway to Fairbanks. After a short distance, this path meets a bridleway heading roughly north-south. Turn right onto the bridleway, following the signpost that directs you back to the Derwent reservoir

Boy, bike, Derwent Reservoir

(although it states that it is a footpath, it really *is* a bridleway). Follow this well-defined bridleway up Cold Side (where, for a little way, it is quite exposed) and back down the side of the two reservoirs, again keeping them on your right. After around five miles, the hardpack track becomes a tarmac road near Jubilee Cottages.
DSF: 10.28 miles (16.54 km).

D **Jubilee Cottages:** Turn right onto the tarmac and drop down the road past the magnificent Derwent Dam. Up the other side and you're back at the car park.
TOTAL DISTANCE: 10.73 miles (17.27 km).

Route Five
DERWENT LOOP

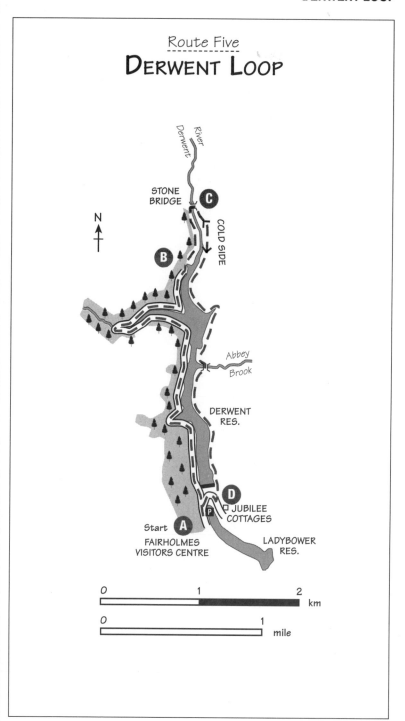

River Derwent

STONE
BRIDGE

C

COLD SIDE

N

B

Abbey
Brook

DERWENT
RES.

D

JUBILEE
COTTAGES

P

Start **A**

FAIRHOLMES
VISITORS CENTRE

LADYBOWER
RES.

0   1   2
km

0   1
mile

Route Six

LADYBOWER

Total Distance: 16.19 miles (26.05 km)

Off-road: 7.95 miles (12.79 km) (49%)

Time taken: 3-4 hours

OS Map: Outdoor Leisure Map 1, *Dark Peak*

Start: Fairholmes Visitor Centre (GR SK173893)

Rail Access: Hope station is a fine place to start the ride if you don't have a car.

Difficulty Ratings

Technical: ●●●○○

Fitness: ●●●●○

The area around the Ladybower reservoir boasts what may be the highest concentration of mountain bikers in the Peaks, luckily it also has a massive amount of well-marked trails and once you leave the car park at the water's edge you'll soon leave the crowds behind. The majority of this ride is well-sheltered and there's a longish road section which takes in some nice picturesque villages, so although quite long there are plenty of places to relax. Highlights are the smooth run down Hagg Down, and the fantastic final descent, again on Hagg Side, which is fast and twisty with a surface that varies from challengingly rocky to superfast smooth. It's perfect – just watch out for the walkers that share your path and the road at the bottom.

The Route

A   **Fairholmes Visitor Centre:** Turn left (S) out of the car park, following the tarmac road until you reach a smaller car park on your right. Just past the car park a gate marks the start of a tree-lined bridleway that climbs the hill. Note that the bridleway is marked by an old signpost reading, 'Public Footpath. Old Pack Rd to Glossop.'
DISTANCE SO FAR (DSF): 0.85 miles (1.37 km).

B   **Bridge End car park:** Take the bridleway and head up Hagg Side for a tiring but perfectly rideable climb on a wide forest road. Ignore all gates until you reach the top. The climb ends at a junction with a bridleway running roughly north-south.
DSF: 1.52 miles (2.45 km)

C   **Hagg Side:** Take the left (S) which is signposted for Ladybower Reservoir. A short grassy climb takes you up to a gate on the horizon. Head through the gate and follow the left track (signposted 'bridleway to Crookhill Farm and Derwent Valley') for a fantastic grassy down that ends at Crookhill farm.
DSF: 3.05 miles (4.91 km).

D   **Crookhill Farm:** Pass through the farmyard and bear left to descend on road to meet the reservoir road.
DSF: 3.39 miles (5.46 km)

E   **Reservoir road:** Turn right (S) onto the road, taking the first left (E) to cross the reservoir. Take the next right turn onto the A6013 to cross the reservoir again. Continue down the A6013 looking out for the first right downhill after the Yorkshire Bridge pub, signposted 'Thornhill'.
DSF: 5.44 miles (8.75 km).

F   **Yorkshire Bridge:** Head down the hill, cross Yorkshire Bridge, turning left at the bottom, continue until you

reach the next little village, Thornhill, looking out for the telephone box.
DSF: 6.73 miles (10.83 km).

G   **Thornhill:** In Thornhill take the right turn just before the red telephone box (signposted 'Not Suitable For Motors') into Carr Lane. Continue gently uphill until you reach Aston. As the road begins to drop, look out for a right turn uphill signposted 'Win Hill and Hope Cross'.
DSF: 7.93 miles (12.76 km).

H   **Aston:** Head uphill for a muddy off-road climb past Edge Farm. The track levels off and follows the contour of Win Hill until it reaches a junction with the wide bridleway close to the side of the wood at Wooler Knoll.
DSF: 9.43 miles (15.18 km).

I   **Wooler Knoll:** Turn left onto the wide sandy track and ride down to meet the Roman Road at a gate.
DSF: 10.27 miles (16.53 km)

J   **Roman Road:** Turn right onto the Roman Road and follow it as it climbs steadily upwards before taking you down for a long and rocky descent. When the track finally levels off, you will be at a right turn onto tarmac taking you further downhill, over Rowlee Bridge and finally up a short but steep climb to meet the A57.
DSF: 12.62 miles (20.31 km).

K   **A57:** Head straight across the A57 and take the steep road uphill past Rowlee Farm on the twisty tarmac road which turns into hardpack, to arrive at a crossroads with another bridleway.
DSF: 13.62 miles (21.92 km).

L   **Woodcock Coppice:** Take the left turn signposted 'Public Bridleway to Lockerbrook & Derwent Reservoir.' After a brief climb, it's downhill to the reservoir.

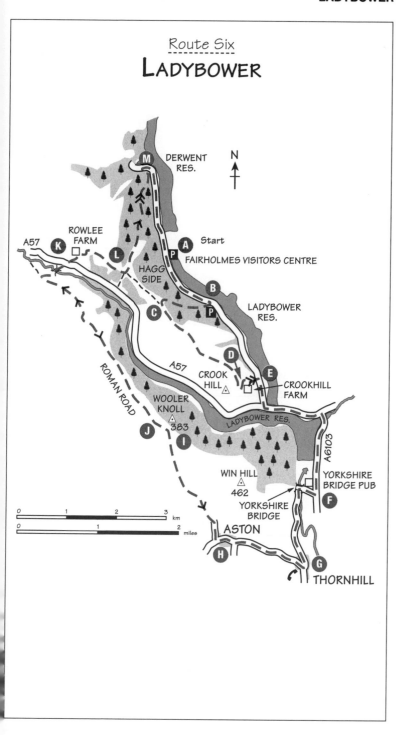

Route Six
LADYBOWER

This fantastic descent starts smooth and fast, crosses two shallow streams before becoming increasingly steep and rocky towards the bottom where it meets the road.

DSF: 15.03 miles (24.19 km).

M   **Reservoir Road:** Turn right on the tarmac and it's just a quick spin back to the car park.

TOTAL DISTANCE: 16.19 miles (26.05 km).

Route Seven
DISLEY

Total Distance: 8.18 miles (13.16 km)
Off Road: 5.45 miles (8.77 km) (67%)
Time taken: 2 hours
OS Map: Outdoor Leisure 1, *Dark Peak*
Start: Strines Station (GR SK978864)
Rail Access: Try Strines Station.

Difficulty Ratings
Technical: ●●●○○
Fitness:　●●●●○

If you're a golf fan, you'll love this ride, as it takes in two of this area's finest courses, so watch out for flying balls. *Fore!* Alternatively, if you love seeing ostriches in the Peak District – and I know there are some of you out there – this is also the ride for you, as there is an ostrich farm just opposite The Banks. It is well worth taking a breather here so you can watch these, the world's largest birds, at play. Like many other rides included in this book, we've kept the climbing, on road and hardpack. Take care not to miss the entrance to the off-road section opposite Woodend Fold, as it is some-times neglected and can become very overgrown. As for downhill fun, the stretches along Black Lane and the Bridleway down to Bottom's Hall are seriously *Waaargh*, and will give any suspension a work-out if approached with atti-tude. Ride carefully.

The Route

A   **Strines Station:** Roll down the cobbled station approach road, then follow the road uphill until you reach the T-junction with the B6101. Turn left.
DISTANCE SO FAR (DSF): 0.37 miles (0.60 km).

B   **B6101:** Turn left onto the B6101 and follow it for 0.40 miles until you reach a house on the left called 'Woodend Fold.' Opposite there is a small lay-by and a narrow track leading into the bushes marked with a sign depicting a horse. This is the start of the bridleway.
DSF: 0.77 miles (1.24 km).

C   **Woodend Fold:** Turn right onto the narrow bridleway and follow it until you come out beside Strines Paper Mill.
DSF: 1.45 miles (2.33 km).

D   **Strines Paper Mill:** Turn left onto tarmac and follow the road mostly uphill for over a mile, straight over the B6101, and up the road on the other side. At the top, follow the road round to the left past Higher Hague Fold Farm, where the road becomes a hardpack track, until you meet Brook Bottom Road.
DSF: 2.69 miles (4.33 km).

E   **Brook Bottom Road:** Go straight across Brook Bottom Road and ride uphill on hardpack, continue along the track until you arrive at the club house on Castle Edge Road.
DSF: 3.32 miles (5.34 km).

F   **The Club House:** Turn left onto Castle Edge Road. Follow it for a little over half a mile on tarmac, then hardpack for the last 100 metres. Look out for a left turn at the crossroads near the quarry (which looks like a small farm).
DSF: 3.95 miles (6.36 km).

G   **The Disused Quarry:** Turn left and follow the road on an upwards incline, (hardpack then soil) until you reach the first big left. This is Black Lane.
DSF: 4.28 miles (6.89 km).

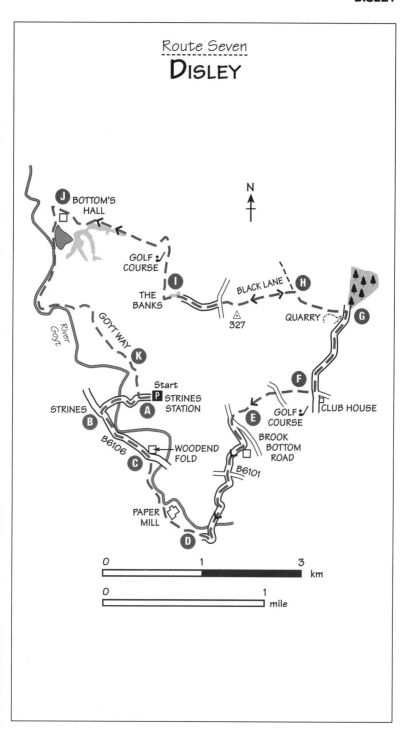

Route Seven
DISLEY

N

J BOTTOM'S HALL

GOLF COURSE

I THE BANKS

BLACK LANE H

River Goyt

GOYT WAY

327

QUARRY

G

K

Start
P STRINES STATION
A

STRINES

B

B6106

C

WOODEND FOLD

F

CLUB HOUSE

E GOLF COURSE

BROOK BOTTOM ROAD

B6101

PAPER MILL

D

| 0 | 1 | 3 |
km

| 0 | 1 |
mile

H   Black Lane: Follow the bridleway uphill, then down a bumpy track. Go straight over a road, and down the rough tarmac track on the other side, which bears to the right through a small wood and turns into rocky singletrack. This brings you out at The Banks opposite the ostrich farm.
DSF: 5.18 miles (8.34 km).

I   The Banks: Turn right on the tarmac, keeping the golf course on your left, until you reach a T-junction. Turn left and follow the road which turns into a bridleway, bringing you out at Bottom's Hall.
DSF: 6.38 miles (10.27 km).

J   Bottom's Hall: Ride past Bottom's Hall and take the first left onto Lakes Road, which becomes the Goyt Way. Follow the bridleway for nearly a mile and a half, keeping the river on your right. At the end of the bridleway, go through a gate and turn right, passing Greenclough Farm House on your right.
DSF: 7.81 miles (12.57 km).

K   Greenclough Farm House: Follow the track down for a quarter of a mile, until you reach a crossroads, where you turn left and find yourself back at the station.
TOTAL DISTANCE: 8.18 miles (13.16 km).

Route Eight

SETT VALLEY

Total Distance: 14.62 miles (23.53 km) *or* 16.88 miles (27.17 km)

Off-road: 12.00 miles (19.31 km) (82% *or* 71%)

Time taken: 3½ hours

OS Map: Outdoor Leisure 1, *Dark Peak*

Start #1: Hayfield Visitor Centre (GR SK036869); **rail access:** not practical.

Start #2: Chinley Station (GR SK038826); **rail access:** easy.

Difficulty Ratings

Technical: ●●●○○

Fitness: ●●●●○

This ride has two possible starts. We set out from Hayfield Visitor Centre which has no rail access but makes for a better ride. We've also included details of an alternative start point at nearby Chinley station for all of you without access to a car – but, be warned: this adds in a nasty bit of tarmac, all up-hill. Wherever you start, you'll find this ride packs in a wide variety of terrain from smile-inducing sand tracks that swoop through the moors to the windswept grass tracks that climb up the side of Lantern Pike. This is a beautiful ride which, despite its numerous ups, rides fairly smoothly through some of the Peak's best scenery. The gravity set will enjoy the wide fast downhill stretch into Birch Vale and the fine drop down from the Shooting Cabins to the A624 on the sandy moorland track. This is one of the sweetest routes in the Peak, pleasantly quiet and full of wide-open spaces.

Note: Be careful not to miss the small stile at point E.

The Route

A **Hayfield Visitor Centre:** Head straight through the car park, across the road and under the A624 via the underpass. Roll down the road and you'll come out by the church with the Twenty Trees Café opposite you. Turn left, cycle over the bridge and take the second right onto Bank Street (i.e. don't end up in the Royal Hotel car park) following the signpost for a campsite. You'll soon reach a sharp left (it's quite easy to miss so look closely) which is the start of Snake Path.
DISTANCE SO FAR (DSF): 0.37 miles (0.60 km).

B **Snake Path:** The start of Snake Path is marked by an old sign which begins, 'This Footpath is dedicated ...' Don't be fooled, this *is* the bridleway you're looking for. The climb up Snake Path starts steeply but the going soon becomes easier. Avoid the misleading track that leads off east near the start of the track and continue to bear left (N) through a series of black 'kissing gates'. Soon you'll be spinning along the sandy track across the moors towards two white shooting cabins.
DSF: 1.60 miles (2.37 km).

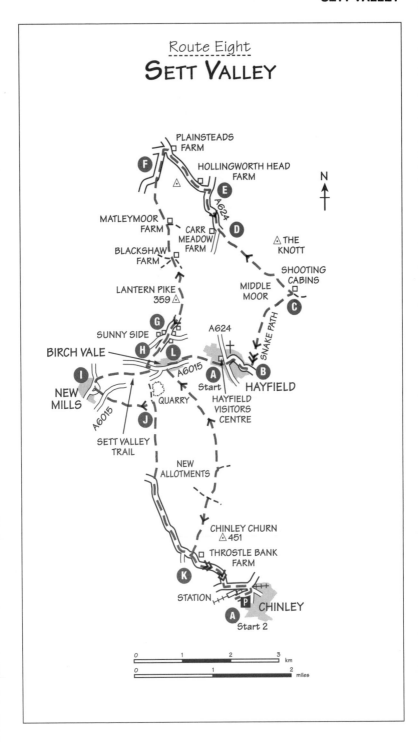

C   **Shooting Cabins:** At the T-junction before the shooting cabins turn left (NW). Continue along this sandy track, descending to meet the A624.
DSF: 2.91 miles (4.68 km).

D   **Car Meadow Farm/A624:** Turn right (N) onto the busy Glossop Road for a tiresome slog upwards until you reach the first turning on your left signposted for Charlesworth.
DSF: 3.46 miles (5.57 km).

E   **Hollingworth Head Farm:** Take this left turn which heads roughly NW until you reach the next left turn at Plainsteads Farm. Take this turn and watch out for the small stile on the first bend (after 0.43 miles).
DSF: 4.59 miles (7.39 km).

F   **Small Stile:** Over the stile and across some whippy singletrack which gets a little wider as you progress. Careful navigation is required around Blackshaw Farm where numerous paths cross; the bridleway is the unsignposted left fork and can just be made out as it climbs gently up the side of Lantern Pike. After this gentle climb you can expect an excellent singletrack descent to Sunny Side where the track gives way to tarmac before you reach a T-junction with another road.
DSF: 6.70 miles (10.78 km).

G   **Sunny Side:** Turn right onto the road then drop down left almost immediately at a signpost for a bridleway. Descend on tarmac for 0.20 miles. As the road takes a hairpin left, you'll spot a stile. Cross this onto a quick rocky downhill through a wood, dropping to a T-junction with Station Road.
DSF: 7.13 miles (11.47 km).

H   **Station Road:** Turn left, across the bridge over the River Sett. Cross the road just after Ellen's Café and join the Sett Valley Trail on the right. Continue (W) along the Sett Valley Trail until you meet Thornsett Road.
DSF: 8.00 miles (12.87 km).

Winter in The Peak

I   **Thornsett Road:** Turn left onto the road and take the first left which takes you uphill off-road by the side of what looks like a football pitch-cum-building site, to meet the A6015. Turn left, then take the first right onto a bridleway. Follow the bridleway to Gibb Hey farm where you cross a stream and enter a small wood through a small white gate, climbing up through Over Lea farm (you go through their garden, so be polite). Continue upwards to meet a T-junction with Over Hill Road next to a Birch Vale Quarry.
    DSF: 9.09 miles (14.63 km).

J   **Birch Vale Quarry:** Turn right (S) and continue straight down Over Hill Road which is a mix of hardpack and tarmac. As the road looks like it's about to level off, look out for a turn on the left which takes you off-road up a rocky climb through a gate just before Throstle Bank farm.
    DSF: 11.14 miles (17.93 km).

K   **Throstle Bank Farm:** Take the track to the left which

heads uphill and off-road. Continue up this path which climbs gently for a little over a mile, go straight across the signposted crossroads and begin a long fast down. After a little over a mile you'll meet a gate after which the track becomes a badly tarmacked road (Marland Rd), continue with a little more care to the bottom of this road where it meets the A6015 in Birch Vale.
DSF: 13.76 miles (22.14 km).

L   **Birch Vale/A6015:** Head straight over the A6015 and drop down a path onto the Sett Valley Trail. Take a right to head east and it's a quick blast along the hardpack to reach the end of the ride at Hayfield Visitor Centre car park.
TOTAL DISTANCE: 14.62 miles (23.53 km).

The Alternative Start: Chinley Station

A2   **Chinley Station:** Turn left out of the station and cycle a short way along Station Road until you meet the T-junction with Green Lane. Turn left here up a slight hill, over a railway bridge and then left again at the war memorial following the sign for Stubbs Lane. Now you have a long slog up the tarmac (aptly named 'Over Hill Road' on the Outdoor Leisure Map) climbing for nearly a mile. As the road begins to flatten out, you'll arrive at Throstle Bank Farm which brings you into the ride at point **K** in the above description. This being a circular route you with find yourself at Throstle Bank Farm on the return leg of the journey. At this point, descend back into Chinley and retrace your route to the station.
TOTAL EXTRA DISTANCE: 2.26 miles (3.64 km) = 1.13 miles (1.82 km) each way.

Route Nine
WHALEY BRIDGE

Total Distance: 8.71 miles (14.02 km)

Off-road: 4.40 miles (7.08 km) (51%)

Time taken: 2½ – 3 hours

OS Map: Outdoor Leisure 1, *Dark Peak*

Start: Whaley Bridge Station car park (GR SK011816)

Rail Access: Head for the rather obvious Whaley Bridge Station.

Difficulty Ratings

Technical: ●●●○○

Fitness:　 ●●●○○

This is a route for those of you who enjoy a variety of scenery and terrain in your rides, starting out from the busy centre of Whaley Bridge (home of The Bike Factory, which is well worth a look), before heading out onto the hills. The route starts out gently along the side of the Peak Forest Canal; look on this as the warm up for a long climb on road up to Clough Head. After this, it's fairly easy going and mainly off-road with some fun to be had on the downhills which vary from narrow tree-lined tracks to wide and fast rock-strewn fields. Look at it as the mountain biking equivalent of a Kellogg's variety pack – something for everyone.

The Route

A   **Whaley Bridge Station car park:** Turn left out of the car park and roll down to the busy A5004. Turn left onto the A5004 and almost immediately right once you're on it. Once across, turn left onto Canal Street and follow the road around to the right, following the sign for the public car park (which is an alternative start point). **DISTANCE SO FAR (DSF):** 0.12 miles (0.19 km).

B   **Canal car park:** Just before Bingswood Avenue, at a direction post, turn left and head North to start following the canal. After a short distance, go over a foot-bridge – or ride cautiously over the weir. At just under half a mile (0.46 miles) you come to the canal equivalent of a T-junction. Cross the foot-bridge here (sign-posted for the Midshires Way) and keep to the left to continue heading North. About a third of a mile further on, having passed under the concrete road

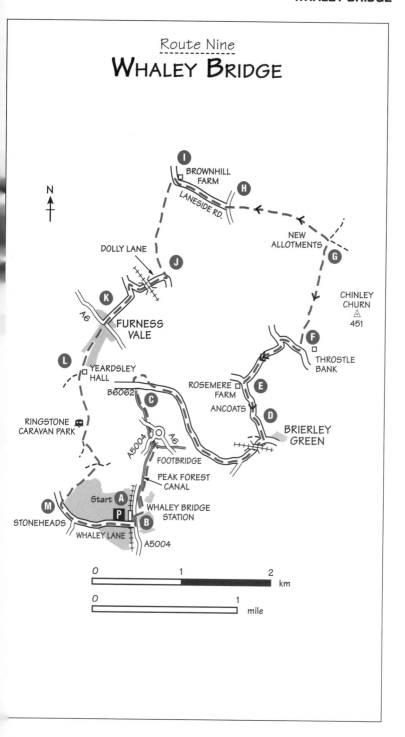

Route Nine
WHALEY BRIDGE

N

I BROWNHILL FARM
H
LANESIDE RD.

NEW ALLOTMENTS
G

DOLLY LANE
J

CHINLEY CHURN
△ 451

K
A6
FURNESS VALE

F
THROSTLE BANK

L

YEARDSLEY HALL
B6062
ROSEMERE FARM
E

C
ANCOATS
D

RINGSTONE CARAVAN PARK
A5004
A6
BRIERLEY GREEN

FOOTBRIDGE

PEAK FOREST CANAL

Start A
P
WHALEY BRIDGE STATION
M B

STONEHEADS
WHALEY LANE
A5004

0   1   2
                              km

0   1
                              mile

bridges, the B6062 crosses the canal by way of an old stone bridge. Ignore the footpath before the bridge. Instead, immediately *after* the bridge, turn right (E) to a short stretch of a minor tarmac road, which leads directly up to the B6062.
DSF: 1.01 miles (1.63 km).

C   **B6062:** Turn left (E) onto the B6062 and follow it into Buxworth until it takes you under a railway bridge. After the bridge, take the second left (N) (with a sign reading 7.5T).
DSF: 2.20 miles (3.54 km).

D   **Brierley Green:** Climb up the road until you reach Rosemere Farm at the top (named **Ancoats** on the OS map) At this point you're going to turn right to continue the long climb uphill.
DSF: 2.61 miles (4.20 km).

E   **Ancoats:** Turn right (NE) to begin this testing tarmac climb. As the road finally levels off (after 0.44 miles), take the sharp right to continue uphill (for a further 0.20 miles) until you reach a rough mud track on the left.
DSF: 3.25 miles (5.23 km).

F   **Throstle Bank:** Climb this initially steep, rough and often muddy track up through a gate. Continue up along the side of Chinley Churn and through three more gates until you meet a crossroads of bridleways at New Allotments, where the hill levels out.
DSF: 4.05 miles (6.52 km).

G   **New Allotments:** Take the left fork (NW) downhill on this wide rocky path. Watch out for the gate halfway down. Carry on through the gate onto the narrower path which eventually brings you out facing Laneside Road (this last section is often wet).
DSF: 4.82 miles (7.76 km).

H **Laneside Road:** Go straight ahead and roll down this fairly steep road until you reach Brownhill Farm where you will see a signpost for a bridleway on your left. **DSF:** 5.23 miles (8.42 km).

I **Brownhill Farm:** Take the signposted bridleway on the left (S) which is a narrow tree-lined hardpack track (ignore side turnings) that eventually brings you out at a junction with Dolly Lane. **DSF:** 5.94 miles (9.56 km).

J **Dolly Lane:** Take the right turn and follow the road around under the railway bridge, following the signs for Furness Vale. Ride over the train track in Furness and up to meet the A6. **DSF:** 6.63 miles (10.67 km).

K **Furness Vale – A6:** Go straight across the A6 and continue uphill onto Yeardsley Lane until it finally peters out. **DSF:** 6.90 miles (11.10 km).

L **Yeardsley Hall:** Continue along the untarmacked road following it around to the left. Keeping Ringstone caravan park on your right, drop down a narrow track to meet a gate. Through the gate, across a small stream, and you're in a big field. Follow the track around the edge of the field, keeping the new housing estate on the left. Don't go through the first gate that you come to – just keep on until Stoneheads, where the path passes through a couple of houses to meet Whaley Lane. **DSF:** 8.13 miles (13.08 km).

M **Stoneheads – Whaley Lane:** Turn left onto Whaley Lane and you'll arrive back at Whaley Bridge station. **TOTAL DISTANCE:** 8.71 miles (14.02 km).

Route Ten

HAYFIELD – EDALE LOOP

Total Distance: 14.28 miles (21.10 km)

Off-road: 8.94 miles (14.37 km) (63%)

Time taken: 4 hours

OS Map: Outdoor Leisure 1, *Dark Peak*

Start: Edale Station car park (GR SK124853)

Rail Access: you work it out.

Difficulty Rating

Technical: ●●●●●

Fitness:　 ●●●●●

This is one of the Peak's all time classic rides, including some tough climbs and a couple of fantastic descents, it might not seem long at a little over fourteen miles but it packs in loads of hard-core off-road terrain and over 790m of climbing. Be warned, this ride crosses some exposed terrain – so go properly equipped; it gets cold and windy quickly around here. Out of Edale and you're soon on the crazy climb up Jacob's Ladder – only the best climbers will make this one. The descent down from Edale cross is fast and rocky and will really test out your bike's suspension, or your knees. Once in Hayfield, you have a good selection of eateries, but the smart money is on the Twenty Trees Café. The best downs are left for the second half of the ride where there's the rocky (and getting rockier) descent into Roych Clough, at the bottom of which there's an ideal site to pause for a break before the climb back out. The next highlight has to be Chapel Gate Track, which is a seriously fast rutted downhill. There's a gate in the middle of what would otherwise be one of the Peak's best downhill tracks: watch out for it and, if you have the energy, get someone to open/close it for you, and enjoy.

The Route

A   **Edale Station car park:** Turn right out of car park to head west through Barber Booth taking the right turn signposted to Upper Booth. Follow this road, which becomes hardpack past Lee Farm until you reach a bridge/ford over the stream at the foot of Jacob's Ladder.
DISTANCE SO FAR (DSF): 0.90 miles (1.45 km).

B   **Jacob's Ladder:** Cross the bridge or ford the stream before turning left through a gate onto the infamous Jacob's Ladder. The steps straight ahead are on a footpath; ignore these and take the zigzag track to the left for a testing climb/push.
DSF: 2.85 miles (4.59 km).

C   **Edale Cross:** Follow the track (W) across the crossroads with the Pennine Way, down and then up to Edale Cross gate which is on the skyline. Remain on the rocky track which descends to join with South Head Farm road.
DSF: 4.41 miles (7.10 km).

D   **South Head Farm Road:** Descend on this tarmac road following it round to the right for 1.17 miles until you reach the T-junction with Kinder Road. Take a left along this road which eventually descends into Hayfield (0.80 miles). Turn left at the bottom of this road.
DSF: 6.38 miles (10.27 km).

E   **Hayfield:** Once you're in Hayfield centre, head for the church. Opposite is the Twenty Trees Café. From the Twenty Trees, head SE up the hill. Turn left at 'Antiques and Pine', a shop with a massive clock on the wall, and immediately right along Highgate Road continuing uphill until you reach the dirt track on your left opposite The Firs.
DSF: 7.31 miles (11.76 km).

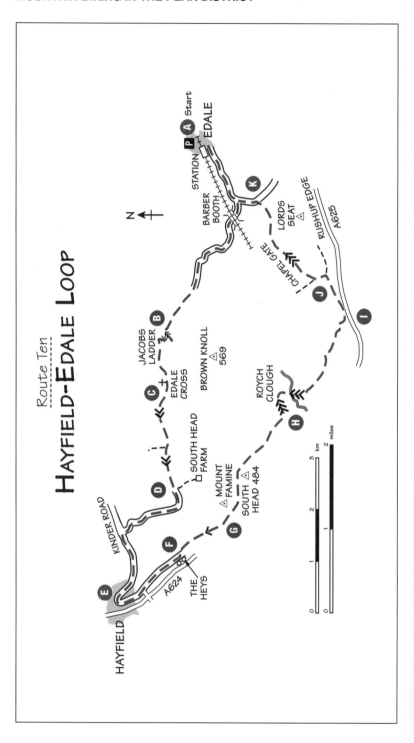

Route Ten

HAYFIELD-EDALE LOOP

F   **The Firs:** Take the walled track on the left and climb for 0.77 miles to reach the gate at Mount Famine. **DSF:** 8.08 miles (13.00 km).

G   **Mount Famine:** Go straight on through the double gates. Follow the obvious track around to the left, then around to the right at South Head and downhill through a series of gates. **DSF:** 9.70 miles (15.61 km).

H   **Roych Clough:** Follow the main path through the left gate, follow the rough track down to Roych Clough. Head through the gate, cross the stream and begin the climb up towards the A625. The track soon eases off and, after a nasty climb on steep broken ground, becomes an easy climb on hard-packed sandy ground. **DSF:** 12.18 miles (19.60 km).

The descent into Roych Clough

I   **A625:** At the Junction with the A625 turn left (NE) using the concessionary bridleway on the moor side of the wall which takes you into a sunken bridleway which is a technical and rocky climb for 0.50 miles and through a gate at the top. **DSF:** 12.68 miles (20.41 km).

J **Top of Sunken Bridleway:** A signpost marks the junction of the paths, take the left fork (NE) signposted for Barber Booth. The track bears right around the base of Lord's Seat before descending on a rough broken tarmac trail (Chapel Gate Track). At the bottom, head through the gate and continue along the track to the T-junction with the road.
DSF: 13.38 miles (21.53 km).

K **Barber Booth:** Turn left (N) onto the road and follow it round through Barber Booth back into the car park at Edale.
TOTAL DISTANCE: 14.28 miles (22.98 km).

Route Eleven

CASTLETON

Total Distance: 8.80 miles (14.16 km)
Off-road: 5.00 miles (8.04 km) (57%)
Time taken: 2½ – 3 hours
OS Map: Outdoor Leisure 1, *Dark Peak*
Start: Castleton car park (GR SK149829)
Rail Access: Hope Station is the nearest option.

Difficulty Ratings
Technical: ●●●●○
Fitness: ●●●○○

This ride uses a short section of the Hayfield Edale Loop, which means it takes in the grin-inducing down of Chapel Gate Track. This ride also takes in the classic views from the top of Mam Tor/Hollins Cross, and the beautiful scenery around Rushup Edge. But be warned – for getting up this high isn't always easy, although we've kept the climbs mainly on tarmac, which includes the famous collapsed road on the other side of Mam Tor. There is also the small matter of the down from Hollins Cross into Castleton which is a monster steep drop straight down the side of the hill. Keep your eyes out for the shallow bombhole in the middle, which can be trouble at speed. It's worth remembering that it gets very cold very quickly on these high, exposed mountainsides, so wear your thermals. Finally, if anyone is a beggar for lung-busting climbs, take a detour into Edale from the bottom of Chapel Gate Track and climb up Cold Side, which turns from a gentle uphill track into a steep off-road push. Ouch!

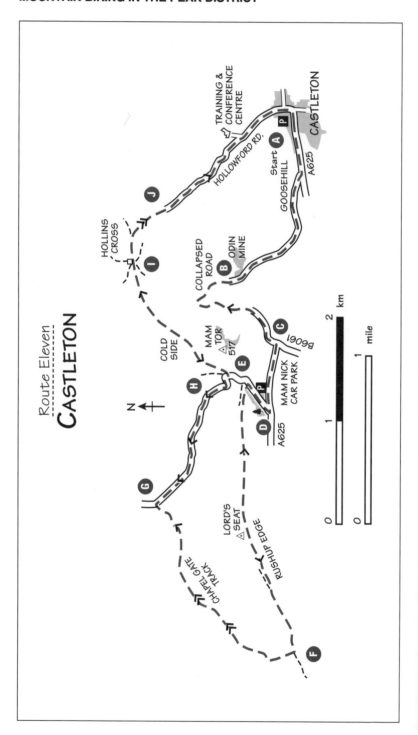

The Route

A   **Castleton car park:** Turn right onto the A625, and follow the road until it ends with a bus turning area at the bottom of the old collapsed road at the foot of Goose Hill.
DISTANCE SO FAR (DSF): 1.16 miles (1.87 km).

B   **Odin Mine:** Simply follow the road up to the top, through the gate and the car park, until you're at the junction with the A625. Turn right.
DSF: 2.13 miles (3.43 km).

C   **A625:** Follow the road for 0.42 miles until you reach the right turn just after Mam Nick car park. Take the right following the sign for Edale and Barber Booth.
DSF: 2.55 miles (4.10 km).

D   **Mam Nick car park:** Go uphill for 0.22 miles until you see the bridleway entrance on your left, just before the brow of the hill. Head through the five-barred gate onto the track that leads up to Rushup Edge.
DSF: 2.77 miles (4.46 km).

E   **Rushup Edge:** Follow the bridleway which initially climbs steeply but soon flattens out. When the bridleway reaches the ridge, stick with the lower track which heads through a gate and across a couple of fields for a long but gentle grassy climb. The track slopes down a little towards the end when it rejoins the main ridge track.
DSF: 4.50 miles (7.24 km).

F   **Chapel Gate Track:** A signpost marks the junction of the paths, take the right fork signposted for Barber Booth. The track bears right around the base of Lord's Seat before descending on a rough broken tarmac track full of ruts and bumps. At the bottom, head through the gate and continue along the track to the T-junction with the road.
DSF: 5.20 miles (8.37 km).

G **Road at bottom of Chapel Gate Track:** Turn right and head uphill for just over a mile. Follow the road that runs up Cold Side until you reach a wooden gate on the left. Go through.
DSF: 6.23 miles (10.03 km).

H **Mam Tor Bus Stop:** Follow the bridleway on a generally more gentle uphill course for a mile, going through a few gates on the way, until you reach Hollins Cross (a large, circular stone.)
DSF: 7.23 miles (11.64 km).

I **Hollins Cross:** Continue straight on past Hollins Cross for a short distance, heading for the blue bridleway arrow that directs you off to the right-hand side of the main track. Follow the fork to a narrow gate, through that to a second gate and through that into a large field. Shortly after the second gate, the path forks to the right. Take the right onto the sunken path and look out for a sharp right turn taking you straight down the side of the hill to meet the gate at the bottom. Through the gate at the bottom and down some rocky singletrack, which brings you out onto Hollowford Road.
DSF: 7.83 miles (12.60km).

A carry near Castleton

J   **Hollowford Road:** Follow this tarmac road straight back into Castleton, making sure that you don't take the turn off for the Conference Centre. Here you meet back up with the A625. Turn right and head back to the car park.
TOTAL DISTANCE: 8.80 miles (14.16 km).

Route Twelve

REDMIRES RESERVOIR

Total Distance: 6.81 miles (10.96 km) *or* 10.65 miles (17.14 km)

Off-road: 3.47 miles (5.58 km) (51%) *or* 5.01 miles (8.06 km) (47%)

Time taken: 1½ hours

OS Map: Outdoor Leisure 1, *Dark Peak*

Start: Redmires Road car park (GR SK269858)

Rail Access: Not really.

Difficulty Ratings

Technical: ●○○○○ *or*
●●●○○

Fitness: ●●○○○ *or*
●●●○○

This ride is suitable for virtually all visitors to the Peak District. To start, park in the Redmires Road car park – easily found if you drive through Lodge Moor. The route is short and sweet, and if you choose not to do the extra section, contains very rideable ascents. The mainly hardpack trail takes you through some pretty forest, past the impressive Ronksley Hall Farm, and across the oh-so-picturesque Rivelin Dam. Only the section of track around Ronksley Farm tends to get muddy, unless you extend your ride up the bridleway to Stanedge Pole. If you do this, however, you will be rewarded with a magnificent view of Stanage Edge and the highly entertaining descent on the same fast track.

If you get hungry en-route, there is a café at the junction of Rails Road and the A6101. However, if it's a nice day, take a picnic and eat out by the reservoir, which you'll find by turning right out of the car park. *Bon appétit!*

The Route

A   **Redmires Road car park:** Head north(ish) out of the car park on the wide forestry track road. Continue straight on along this smooth downhill (ignore the track that heads off to the right) which levels out before a short climb up to meet the A57.
DISTANCE SO FAR (DSF): 1.77 miles (2.85 km).

B   **A57:** Turn right onto the road and roll down the hill. Just around the sharp bend is a small group of houses and a road heading off on the left.
DSF: 2.19 miles (3.52 km).

C   **Onksley Lane:** Turn left and head uphill on this narrow tarmac road. After a steep start the road soon eases up, bringing you to the end of the tarmac at Ronksley Hall farm.
DSF: 2.60 miles (4.18 km).

D   **Ronksley Hall Farm:** Just past the hall a farm track heads off to the right (E) between two stone walls.

Follow the, often muddy, track between the walls until you emerge at a T-junction with a tarmac road.
DSF: 3.20 miles (5.15 km).

E   **The Flash:** Turn right downhill on tarmac following Woodbank road around a sharp left bend to meet Bingley lane (or Rails Road, depending on which sign you believe).
DSF: 3.90 miles (6.28 km).

F   **Bingley Lane/Rails Road:** Turn right downhill to meet a T-junction with the A6101.
DSF: 4.18 miles (6.73 km).

G   **A6101:** Turn right onto the main road (there's a café at this junction if you're hungry already) and continue to meet a junction with the A57. Turn right and head along Manchester Road in a roughly westerly direction until you reach the road over the dam at Rivelin Reservoir on your left.
DSF: 5.25 miles (8.45 km).

H   **Rivelin Dam:** Ride across the dam and follow the road around to the right to cycle uphill through the trees on a wide forestry road. Continue uphill until your track joins Wyming Brook Drive (the track you started out on).
DSF: 6.01 miles (9.67 km).

I   **Wyming Brook Drive**. Turn left to cycle back up the track to arrive at the car park.
TOTAL DISTANCE: 6.81 miles (10.96 km).

The Extra Section

J   **Redmires Road car park:** Turn right out of the car park onto Redmires Road. Continue along the road until you reach the end at which point you will see a wide rocky bridleway heading off uphill through a gate.
DSF: 1.15 miles (1.85 km).

Route Twelve

REDMIRES RESERVOIR

A57

RONKSLEY HALL FARM □ **D** **E** **F** **G**

A6101

B **C** **H**

N

RIVELIN DAMS

I

J **P** **A** Start
REDMIRES ROAD
CAR PARK

K REDMIRES RES.

L △
STANEDGE POLE
435

K   **Bridleway start:** Head off up the hill and keep going until you reach the top. It's quite a gentle climb on a smooth sandy road although the last section after the only gate is a little rockier. At the top, you will see Stanedge Pole. It's time to turn around.
DSF: 1.92 miles (3.09 km).

L   **Stanedge Pole:** Retrace your route to the car park.
TOTAL DISTANCE: 3.84 miles (6.18 km).

Route Thirteen
CASTLETON – ELDON

Total Distance: 9.80 miles (15.77 km)

Off-road: 5.00 miles (8.05 km) (51%)

Time taken: 2½ hours

OS Map: Outdoor Leisure 1, *Dark Peak*

Start: Castleton car park (GR SK149829)

Rail Access: Edale is the nearest station, adding a couple of kilometers (mostly off-road) to each end of the ride.

Difficulty Ratings

Technical: ●●●○○

Fitness: ●●○○○

This is a smashing ride. At a little under ten miles long, it's just the right distance for Sunday riders. All the climbs are on road or hardpack, leaving you free to concentrate on your legs and lungs, rather than on bunny-hopping up boulders. The downs at Oxlow Rake and Dirtlow Rake are both great fun, but be warned, Dirtlow Rake is a beggar for punctures. Cavedale is a completely different kettle of fish, with a middle section so rocky that it is virtually unrideable to mere mortals. Still, the top and bottom sections make it all worthwhile. Keep an eye out for the breathtaking scenery, and the view of Peveril Castle . . . and, of course, the crowds of walkers.

The Route

A **Castleton**: Turn left out of the car park onto the A625, following the road until you reach the church. Turn right here and cycle on up the hill, passing a grass triangle. Bear left here and continue up the increasingly steep hill (ignore the fork down and left). The road eventually flattens out – keep going until you reach a barn on your right.
DISTANCE SO FAR (DSF): 1.92 miles (3.09 km).

B **Dirtlow Rake:** Just after the barn take the track right that leads to a T-junction with the quarry road. (at this point you have the option of turning right and riding 0.70 miles of fast rocky downhill (around 30 mph here) and repeating the last section of the tarmac climb again) To continue, take a left up the quarry road, following it round until you reach a crossroads. Turn left through the gate onto the Limestone Way.
DSF: 2.64 miles (4.25 km).

C **Limestone Way:** Follow the track, keeping the wall on your right. After a short distance the track divides, take the right fork through the gate (do *not* continue over the stile).
DSF: 3.1 miles (4.99 km).

D **Oxlow Rake:** The track climbs slightly, flattens out, then descends along a tree-lined track. Watch out for the two gates along this descent, which may or may not be open. Go through the gate at the bottom and turn left, after a short distance, you'll meet a T-junction with Old Dam Lane. Turn right and freewheel down into the small cluster of houses known as Old Dam.
DSF: 4.45 miles (7.16 km).

MOUNTAIN BIKING IN THE PEAK DISTRICT

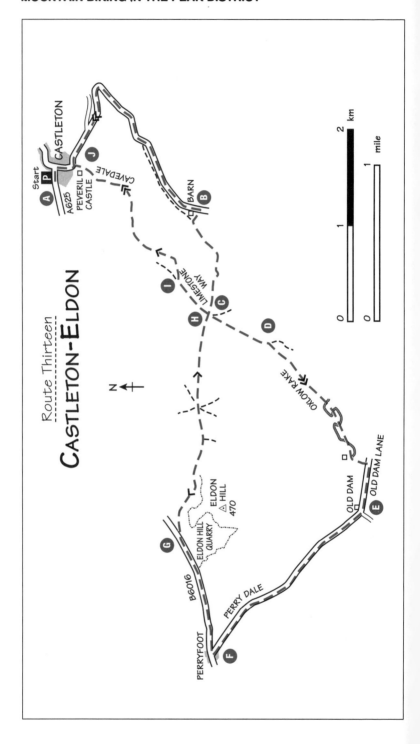

Route Thirteen
CASTLETON-ELDON

E   **Old Dam**: Turn right (NW) at the grass traffic island and continue along the road until you meet a T-junction with the B6061.
DSF: 5.85 miles (9.41 km).

F   **Perryfoot:** Turn right onto the B6061 and climb steadily for 0.80 miles, turning right just after you pass the entrance to Eldon Hill Quarry.
DSF: 6.65 miles (10.70 km).

G   **Eldon Hill Quarry:** This hardpack quarry road begins to climb steadily after a couple of hundred metres. When the road levels out, you will come to a gate. Continue straight on through two more gates until you again arrive at the junction with the Limestone Way.
DSF: 8.15 miles (13.12 km).

H   **Limestone Way:** Turn Left (NE) here, passing through two closely placed gates. Ride down the smooth grass path for 0.28 miles turning right at the first fork which brings you to a small metal gate. Go through the gate into Cavedale.
DSF: 8.43 miles (13.57 km).

Peveril Castle, from Cavedale

I   **Cavedale:** Once through the gate follow the path down to the right. The track soon becomes rocky and extremely technical, easing up toward the bottom.
DSF: 9.62 miles (15.48 km).

J   **Castleton:** Go through the gate at the bottom of Cavedale and roll down the hill back into the centre of Castleton. Left at the church onto the A625 and you've made it home.
TOTAL DISTANCE: 9.80 miles (15.77 km).

Route Fourteen

BRADWELL – SHATTON

Total Distance: 6.85 miles (11.02 km)

Off-road: 4.53 miles (7.29 km) (66.6%)

Time taken: 2 hours

OS Map: Outdoor Leisure 1, *Dark Peak*

Start: Bradwell Church (GR SK175811)

Rail Access: Hope is the nearest station at around three miles from Bradwell.

Difficulty Ratings

Technical: ●●●○○

Fitness:　●●●○○

The most complicated part of this ride is negotiating the seeming labyrinth of Bradwell's back streets, to get yourself onto the bridleway at Bradwell Edge. Once here the ride sticks mainly to mud, grass and hardpack. Bradwell Edge itself is a lung-busting climb on a good old-fashioned mud-and-grass bridleway. On the way back, this same stretch becomes a hair-raising, scream-inducing, singletrack down, for anyone gnarly enough to attack it at speed. Other swift places on this ride include Shatton Lane (tarmac) and Shatton Hall Farm (hardpack).

We parked behind the Food Fair shop in their handy customer car park but, wherever you decide to park, the ride starts from the church on the B6049.

The Route

A   **Bradwell Church:** With the church behind you turn left onto the B6049 and turn left uphill at the first road you come to. Shortly this will bring you to a T-junction, turn left to continue uphill until you reach the turn onto Bessie Lane. This narrow country lane drops down before continuing upwards, deteriorating to muddy hardpack as it climbs. Continue upwards until you reach a gate and stile.
DISTANCE SO FAR (DSF): 0.44 miles (0.71 km).

B   **Bradwell Edge:** Go through the gate and follow the narrow mud track steeply uphill until you reach a small wooden gate. Through the gate, the track widens and the gradient eases. Follow it up to the top, where it bends to the right, keeping the dry stone wall on your left. Head through a metal gate into an open field, and cross the field to the gate opposite where you pick up Brough Lane.
DSF: 0.97 miles (1.56 km).

C   **Brough Lane:** Turn right onto the hardpack road. The road undulates gently, after 0.80 of a mile you will

Route Fourteen
BRADWELL-SHATTON

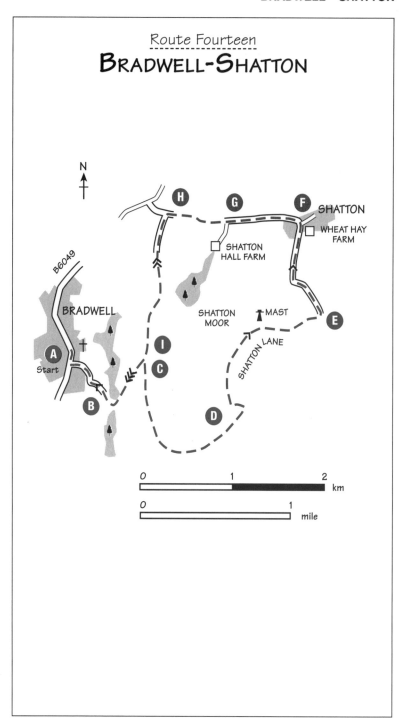

reach a crossroads. Go straight on, following the sign-post directing you to Shatton. Continue until you reach a T-junction, ignore the footpath right/straight-on and take the left fork. Soon you will reach a hardpack road that leads off down to the right between two stone gateposts.
DSF: 2.20 miles (3.54 km).

D   **Shatton Lane:** Head downhill on the wide hardpack road that stays between stone walls until it comes to an end at a gate nearly a mile further on.
DSF: 3.19 miles (5.13 km).

E   **Bottom of Shatton Lane:** Through the gate and head down the tarmac road until it reaches a small group of houses. Look out for the left turn at Wheat Hay Farm.
DSF: 3.87 miles (6.23 km).

F   **Wheat Hay Farm:** Turn left and ride over the ford and follow Townfield Lane until it ends at Shatton Hall Farm (marked Upper Shatton on the OS map). There are two tracks from here, the left one leads to the farm, the right, through a metal gate is the route you want.
DSF: 4.40 miles (7.08 km).

G   **Shatton Hall Farm:** Through the gate and follow the track, ignore the path off to the left and bear right, through a gate, then steeply down to meet two closely placed gates that lead you back onto tarmac.
DSF: 4.80 miles (7.72 km).

H   **Brough Lane (Bottom):** Onto the tarmac, take the left turn uphill. The tarmac soon becomes a lengthy hardpack climb, steep at first and eventually easing off to just plain tiring. Keep on going until you are nearly at the top and you'll see a gate on the right that you should remember from earlier in the day, leading you across a field to a metal gate on the horizon.
DSF: 5.88 miles (9.46 km).

I   **Brough Lane (Top):** Through the gate, and now it's just a question of retracing your steps back to the start. Head up to the gate on the horizon 50 metres away. Go through that and follow the track that takes you down on tight twisty singletrack across Bradwell Edge. Through the gate at the bottom and back onto tarmac for the final drop down into Bradwell.
TOTAL DISTANCE: 6.85 miles (11.02 km).

Descending Bradwell Edge

Route Fifteen

TOTLEY MOOR

Total Distance: 7.29 miles (11.73 km)

Off-road: 5.00 miles (8.05 km) (69%)

Time taken: 2 hours

OS Map: Outdoor Leisure 1, *Dark Peak* and Outdoor Leisure 24, *White Peak*

Start: Longshaw Estate car park (GR SK266800)

Rail Access: There are stations at Grindleford and Totley.

Difficulty Ratings

Technical: ●●●○○

Fitness: ●●●○○

This is one of the cooler rides we know, it's got a bit of everything. There are some nice smooth sections through great scenery, plenty of the fast downhill fun stuff and, unlike many Peak District rides, there are trees too. The best sections are undoubtedly the descent off Totley Moor and the singletrack ride around Wimble Holme Hill, which is an easy trail but has the novelty of a long drop-off to the side should something go awry. From here on, there's the excellent drop through Blacka Plantation which takes you along a steep and twisting narrow track. The wood is full of trails and is well worth an afternoon's exploration if you've got the time. To end the route off, there's the more sedate ride along Houndkirk Road which is something of an off-road motorway across the moor. All in all this is a fine ride made up of several fast and furious sections linked together by some mellow trails, this one will definitely draw you back to explore further.

The Route

A   **Longshaw Estate car park:** Turn right out of the car park and cycle up the hill until the road meets the B6450 at a sort of 'V' version of a T-junction. The bridleway across Totley Moor is just across the road heading almost due east through a five-barred gate. **DISTANCE SO FAR (DSF):** 0.37 miles (0.60 km).

B   **B6055/B6450/Totley Moor:** Head through the gate and ride across the moor on the wide sandy track (be warned it can get pretty wet). Just beyond the air shaft a path joins the main track from the left, at this point (after 0.86 miles on the track) be careful to cycle across the footpath rather than joining it. The bridleway is not as clear as the path itself at this point and drops slightly to the left, soon becoming a very narrow track. Once the bridleway meets the main track again, take the right upper track downwards to descend *nearly* to the gate at the bottom. Just before you reach the gate look out for a track leading off to the left, there are two

and the one you want is the lower of the two that heads off around the edge of Wimble Holme Hill.
DSF: 1.86 miles (2.99 km).

C **Wimble Holme Hill:** Follow the narrow track as it follows the contour around the side of Wimble Holme Hill. The track descends slightly to meet a small five-barred gate into a field. Head through the gate and ride up the grassy path that follows the fence. Keep going up this gentle climb until you reach a metal five-barred gate on the right.
DSF: 2.22 miles (3.57 km).

D **Metal Gate:** Head through the gate on the right onto the rocky track that leads you downhill to meet a T-junction and a gap in the wall that is the start of your next track.
DSF: 2.56 miles (4.12 km).

E **Lenny Hill:** Through the gateless gateposts and into Blacka Plantation, follow the main path downhill through the trees for a great twisting descent on a narrow path. It's quite steep at first, levels out and then drops steeply to the stream at the bottom.
DSF: 2.91 miles (4.68 km).

F **Blacka Plantation:** Cross the stream and turn right onto the wider path that follows the river downstream. Join the tarmac at the end of the track and follow it round up Whitelow Road until you reach the A625. (As an alternative, you could turn left for a challenging off-road climb through the trees, again reaching the A625.) The road, if you take it is an easy but lengthy climb.
DSF: 4.39 miles (7.06 km).

G **A625:** Turn right onto the A625 and then take the first left onto Sheephill Road. Cycle uphill, across a stream, until you see the bridleway signposted on your left.
DSF: 4.97 miles (8.00 km).

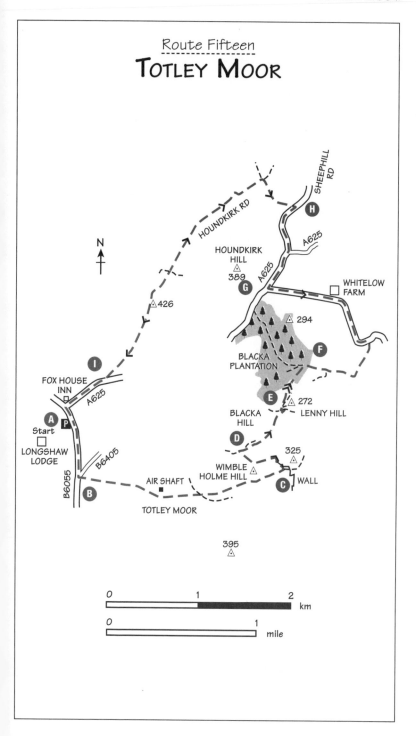

Route Fifteen
TOTLEY MOOR

H   **Sheephill Rd/bridleway:** Go through the gate and cycle up the wide stony path across Houndkirk Moor. After about a quarter of a mile, the track is crossed by another heading NE-SW. Turn left onto this sandy, off-road motorway. It's a smooth climb for nearly a mile before the track descends towards the A625. Towards the bottom of this fast descent, you'll come to a gate. Through this and you're soon at the road.
DSF: 6.89 miles (11.09 km).

I   **A625:** Turn right, downhill, onto the A625 and take the first left at the Fox House Inn. Roll down the road and you'll see the Longshaw Estate car park on your right.
TOTAL DISTANCE: 7.29 miles (11.73 km).

Route Sixteen

BUXTON

Total Distance: 14.74 miles (23.72 km)

Off-road: 4.70 miles (7.56 km) (32%)

Time taken: 2½ – 3 hours

OS Map: Outdoor Leisure 24, *White Peak*

Start: Buxton Station car park (GR SK060738)

Rail Access: The clever money is on Buxton Station. If you're coming by car, the station is a good place to park with an all day ticket costing a couple of pounds.

Difficulty Ratings

Technical: ●●○○○

Fitness: ●●●○○

Bang in the middle of the Peak District, and curiously not actually in it at all, lies the once-prosperous spa town of Buxton. Its central location and big town status (by Peak standards) should make Buxton the ideal base for a spot of mountain biking, but a strange lack of bridleways makes it a something of a disappointment. In fact, there is really only one route to choose from. Good job it's a good one then ... This pleasant circuit shouldn't present the newcomer with too many problems and it packs in enough fun sections to keep everyone entertained. It doesn't take long to get out of Buxton centre and into some fine scenery. The first half of the ride contains the more technical riding with an enjoyable trail around the side of Ladder Hill. On the second section, the trail through Goyt Forest is smooth and fast and is followed by a pleasant stretch of road up to Derbyshire Bridge. Climbing up the rocky road from Derbyshire Bridge may be a pain but the descent is more than worth it, dropping down for two-thirds of a mile to emerge in Burbage, a short stretch of road away from the start point.

The Route

A **Buxton Station car park:** Turn right out of the car park and head down the hill to the first roundabout. Head straight across to reach a second roundabout and turn right uphill onto the A5004, Longhill Road. Continue to ride up the A5004 for about a mile. Just beyond Cold Springs Farm the road bends sharply to the left. Leave the road here by taking a 'right turn', effectively straight on, onto a narrow Roman road.
DISTANCE SO FAR (DSF): 1.42 miles (2.29 km).

B **A5004/Roman road:** Climb up this initially steep track onto the open moor and descend to the White Hall Centre where numerous tracks meet.
DSF: 1.73 miles (2.78 km).

C **White Hall Centre:** Cycle past the White Hall Centre and follow the track as it curves downwards to the right. Ignore the road the heads off right towards Combs and head upwards on tarmac towards Wythen Lache just beyond the brow of the hill. Take care not to turn off too early at Wainstones Farm, and look out for the gate on the right just after the farm buildings that leads into a walled track.
DSF: 2.60 miles (4.18 km).

D **Wythen Lache:** Head through the gate and follow the track between the walls, through a second gate and the track heads across open fields. This track ends at another gate. Head through it to drop down past Thorny Lee on a brief section of tarmac. Turn left when it meets a road uphill. Go through a gate and onto a rutted stony road (Long Lane). Follow this track until you emerge at a T-junction with Old Road.
DSF: 4.45 miles (7.16 km).

E **Elnor Lane Farm/Old Rd:** Turn right and ride down Old Road into the south edge of Whaley Bridge. Take

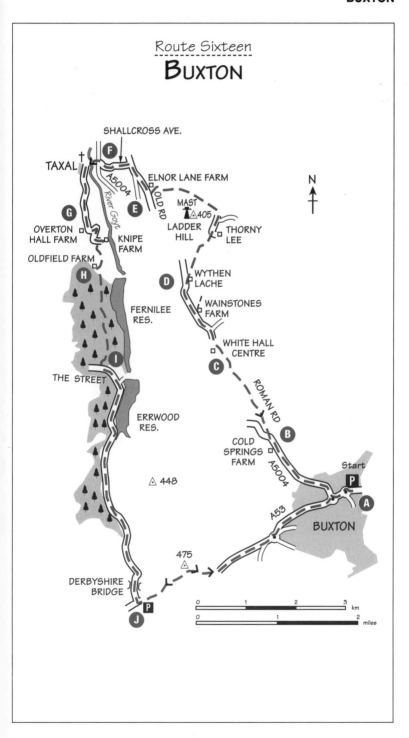

Route Sixteen
BUXTON

SHALLCROSS AVE.

F

TAXAL

A5004

ELNOR LANE FARM

OLD RD

River Goyt

E

N

MAST
△405

LADDER
HILL

THORNY
LEE

G

OVERTON
HALL FARM

KNIPE
FARM

OLDFIELD FARM

H

D

WYTHEN
LACHE

WAINSTONES
FARM

FERNILEE
RES.

WHITE HALL
CENTRE

C

I

THE STREET

ROMAN RD

ERRWOOD
RES.

B

COLD
SPRINGS
FARM

△ 448

A5004

Start
P

A

A53

BUXTON

475
△

DERBYSHIRE
BRIDGE

P

J

0		1		2		3	
							km

0 ———— 1 ———— 2
miles

the second left into Shallcross Avenue. Follow the road up past Shallcross Hall Farm and then descend to meet the busy A5004. Cross the road and head into the large lay-by on the other side.
DSF: 5.37 miles (8.64 km).

F **A5004/Lay-by:** Take the narrow track that leads steeply downwards from the lay-by and ford (or bridge) the River Goyt at the bottom. It's a steep climb out of the valley through a churchyard up to Taxal. At the top turn left and follow the tarmac road climbing gently upwards until you reach a T-junction at Overton Hall Farm.
DSF: 6.39 miles (10.28 km).

G **Overton Hall Farm:** Turn left to head downhill, following the road around to the right on a hairpin bend to reach a gate at Madscar Farm. Go through the gate and down a steep track to the stream at the bottom of Mill Clough. Go through the gate and climb up the track for about 100 metres before taking another right turn through a gate just before Knipe Farm. Climb up the (often muddy) track across the field to another gate. Through the gate and onto a walled track that takes you past a roofless barn, here the track divides, keep to the lower of the two and head straight on to reach Oldfield Farm. If this all seems a bit complicated, just remember to head in a roughly southerly direction.
DSF: 7.33 miles (11.80 km).

H **Oldfield Farm:** Cycle through the farmyard and bear right onto the Forestry Commission road which is signposted 'Hoo Moor'. Continue along this hardpack forest road through the trees until you emerge at a T-junction with 'The Street'.
DSF: 8.57 miles (13.79 km).

I **The Street:** Turn left and ride down the road following it around the side of Errwood Reservoir. After the brief drop down to the reservoir, it's a gradual climb up to the Visitor Centre at Derbyshire Bridge.

DSF: 11.69 miles (18.81 km).

J   **Derbyshire Bridge:** Turn left off the road onto the rocky track that is signposted to Buxton. The rocky track climbs for just over two-thirds of a mile before descending for almost the same distance. The track becomes a tarmac road in Burbage and continues to descend. Follow it down, fork left at the traffic lights to roll down into Buxton on the A53. Head straight across both roundabouts to reach your starting point at Buxton Station.

TOTAL DISTANCE: 14.74 miles (23.72 km).

Route Seventeen

MACCLESFIELD FOREST

Total Distance: 13.24 miles (21.30 km)

Off-road: 5.88 miles (9.46 km) (56%)

Time taken: 3 hours

OS Map: Outdoor Leisure 24, *White Peak*

Start: Macclesfield Forest car park (GR SK961711)

Rail Access: Macclesfield station is five kilometres (ish) away if you're coming by train.

Difficulty Ratings

Technical: ●●●○○

Fitness: ●●●●○

This loop takes you away from the crowded trails of Macclesfield Forest, out to the A537 and to the middle of nowhere where the cars are fast, sheep are wild, and Mountain Bikers strangely rare. Most of the climbing is on road during the first half of the ride leaving you with two fantastic descents, one past Clough House, the other through Macclesfield Forest, for the way back. The bridleways through Macclesfield Forest are all concessionary, so try to stick to them, as they criss-cross with footpaths, and it's easy enough to find yourself suddenly going head-to-head with people out walking Rover. Take care! It may be worth popping into the Visitor Centre to check the current layout of the bridleways as they do occasionally change. Finally, be careful going down to Bottom-of-the-Oven, as the ground suddenly falls away... Oh yes, and make sure that you don't miss the turn off for Clough House (it's a bit tricky). *ENJOY!*

The Route

A **Macclesfield Forest car park:** From the car park, turn left on road, passing Ridgegate Reservoir on your left, until you get to the T-junction that's level with the end of the reservoir.
DISTANCE SO FAR (DSF): 0.66 miles (1.06 km).

B **Higher Ridgegate:** Turn right at the T-junction and ride mostly uphill, on tarmac, until you meet the bridleway entrance on your left.
DSF: 1.05 miles (1.69 km).

C **Bridleway through Macclesfield Forest:** Carry on up the hill initially on hardpack, changing into muddy hardpack, and eventually into singletrack for the last fifth of a mile, until you meet the junction with the road near Ashtreetop.
DSF: 2 miles (3.22 km).

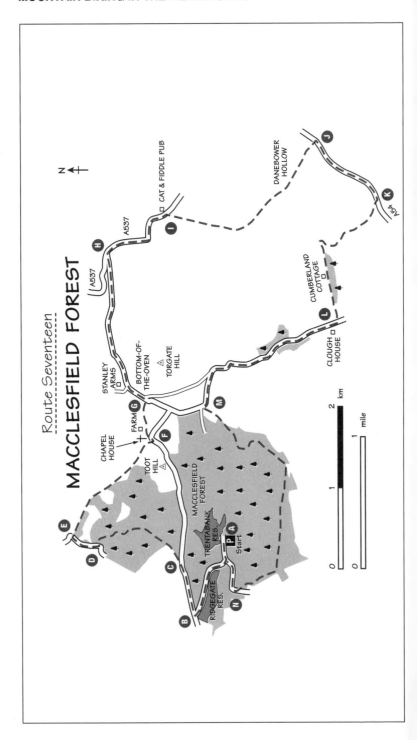

Route Seventeen
MACCLESFIELD FOREST

D **Steep Uphill road:** Turn right up the hill, and keep climbing until the road turns a sharp left. Take the bridleway on your right.
DSF: 2.45 miles (3.94 km).

E **Bridleway to Chapel House Farm:** Head up the bridleway for a brief climb, then it's a lovely fast down on hardpack, until you meet the road by Chapel House Farm.
DSF: 3.46 miles (4.53 km).

F **Chapel House Farm:** Turn left down towards the church, taking the bridleway on your right as the road bends left. Be careful, as the grassy hardpack gives way to a steep, broken-up path ending at a junction with a tarmac road.
DSF: 3.80 miles (6.12 km).

G **Bottom-of-the-Oven:** Turn left and roll down the hill to a T-junction. Turn left, and follow the road to a second T-junction. Turn right, passing the Stanley Arms, following the sign for Buxton. Follow the road up hill to the T-junction with the A537.
DSF: 5.07 miles (8.16 km).

H **A537:** Turn right onto the A537, until you reach the bridleway on your right, opposite the Cat and Fiddle pub.
DSF: 5.71 miles (9.19 km).

I **Cat and Fiddle Pub/Bridleway:** Follow this hardpack/loose stone bridleway until it meets the A54.
DSF: 7.21 miles (11.60 km).

J **A 54:** Turn right and stay on the road for 0.66 miles until you get to a bridleway entrance on the right which slopes upwards. Careful – this is easy to miss.
DSF: 7.87 miles (12.67 km).

K **Sparbent:** The first part of the bridleway is fast,

smooth, hardpack, which leads down to a sharp left and through a gate. Here, the bridleway becomes rocky. Carry on descending, through a second gate and cross the stream at the ford, until you meet the road opposite Clough House.
DSF: 9.19 miles (14.79 km).

L **Clough House:** Turn right and descend to the junction. Turn right and follow the road, passing the lay-by, until you reach a left turn, uphill, signposted for Forest Chapel. Climb to the top of the hill, meeting a bridleway on the left, signposted for Shutingsloe.
DSF: 10.57 miles (17.01 km).

M **Macclesfield Forest Bridleway:** Turn left onto hardpack bridleway. Follow the bridleway arrows through the forest, on the well-marked track until, after a couple of good descents, you reach the road.
DSF: 12.89 miles (20.74 km).

N **Road to car park:** Turn right, and then right again at the T-junction. The car park is on your right.
TOTAL DISTANCE: 13.24 miles (21.30 km).

Route Eighteen

BAKEWELL – STONEY MIDDLETON

Total Distance: 17.09 miles (27.50 km)

Off-road: 8.00 miles (12.88 km) (47%)

Time taken: 4 hours

OS Map: Outdoor Leisure 24, *White Peak*

Start: Bakewell car park (GR SK222686)

Rail Access: not practical, but Padley Chapel if you're desperate.

Difficulty Ratings

Technical: ●●●○○

Fitness: ●●●●○

If you like tarts you'll love Bakewell, the site of this ride. If you really like them then you might want to visit the Rutland Arms where a fortunate accident led to the creation of these tasty treats. If cake history isn't your thing then Bakewell still makes a great base for a few days mountain biking. Let us introduce you to one of our favourite rides . . .

It was almost impossible to decide which way round to ride this route. We honestly recommend that you ride it this way round, but whichever way you go for, you'll get some leg-sapping climbs, and descents which make you scream for more, particularly Black Harry, High Rake, and the oh-so-cool single track through Manners Wood. Basically, this is the Peak District's equivalent of one of those impossible Escher drawings. It's also a very beautiful ride, with smashing scenery that makes the road work pleasant. And there's the added advantage that there are main roads which link the various places on this ride to Bakewell, allowing you a swift escape should conditions suddenly deteriorate.

The Route

A   **Bakewell car park:** Turn left out of the car park, left again onto the B6048 to drop down to the A619. Turn right onto the A619. Take the first left (W) onto Holme Lane and continue until the road runs out and take the right turn (opposite the bridge) off-road and up. **DISTANCE SO FAR (DSF):** 0.54 miles (0.87 km).

B   **Holme Hall:** Cycle up the grassy path until, after several gates, it starts to descend. Descend to meet the Monsal Trail, go straight across and through a field to meet the A6020 at Toll Bar House. **DSF:** 1.81 miles (2.91 km).

C   **Toll Bar House:** Turn right onto the A6020 and continue up to the roundabout. Here take a left (N) onto the B6001 headed for Hassop. In Hassop, look out for a left turn in front of the church. **DSF:** 3.18 miles (5.12 km).

D   **Hassop:** Take the left turn to ride uphill on tarmac to the next right (N) onto the quieter road to Rowland. Head through Rowland, past Top Farm the road surface deteriorates. Look out for the next left turn, which heads off-road and uphill. **DSF:** 4.44 miles (7.15 km).

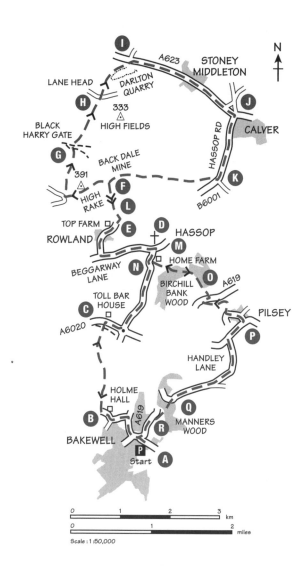

Route Eighteen
BAKEWELL-STONEY MIDDLETON

E   **Rowland:** Cycle/push up the hill through the trees to meet the quarry road at the top.
DSF: 4.93 miles (7.93 km).

F   **High Rake:** Turn left (W) on the wide quarry road which takes you a little further uphill and then down, right around a gravely corner, to meet a gate. Through the gate and it's a smooth down to meet a pair of gates at Black Harry Gate.
DSF: 6.14 miles (9.88 km).

G   **Black Harry Gate:** Head through the gate, then across and through the gate opposite, and up Black Harry Lane. Before long this levels out and descends to meet a crossroads with Middleton Lane.
DSF: 6.82 miles (10.98 km).

H   **Lane Head:** Head straight across the road and down the steep track into Darlton Quarry, continue through the quarry to come out on the A623.
DSF: 7.44 miles (11.97 km).

I   **Darlton Quarry/A623:** Turn right (E) on the A623. Cycle through Stoney Middleton until you reach the large crossroads at Calver. You're going to turn right here.
DSF: 8.87 miles (14.27 km).

J   **Calver/Hassop Road:** Turn right (uphill) onto Hassop Road and continue until you reach a crossroads on the brow of the hill. Turn right here onto the quarry road.
DSF: 9.71 miles (15.62 km).

K   **Back Dale Mine:** Climb up the quarry road until the quarry is on your right – you should recognise this from earlier on the ride (point F). At the top of the climb, two paths descend on the left; take the narrower left-hand track (marked with a large rock). The singletrack path snakes through the trees for 0.49 miles, coming out at a T-junction with a farm road.
DSF: 11.63 miles (18.72 km).

L **Rowland:** Turn right (SW) through Rowland to the T-junction with Beggarway Lane. Turn left and cycle into Hassop.
DSF: 12.89 miles (20.74 km).

M **Hassop:** Turn right onto the B6001 following the signpost for Bakewell. Almost immediately on your left you will see Home Farm and just beyond this a track, again on the left, marked 'Unsuitable For Motors', head up here.
DSF: 13.01 miles (20.94 km).

N **Home Farm:** Follow the track slightly uphill and then it's a rocky down to ford a stream, up the other side and straight on to meet the A619.
DSF: 14.01 miles (22.55 km).

O **A619:** Turn right onto the A619 and almost immediately take the next left (just before a short parking area on the right) which takes you uphill on a rocky off-road track through the trees. Climb to the top where you meet a T-junction with a rough farm road. Turn left into Pilsey and take the first right to meet the B6048.
DSF: 14.82 miles (23.85 km).

P **Pilsey/B6048:** Turn right out of Pilsey onto the B6048 and take the first left onto Handley Lane for a tiring road climb. Just as you crest the hill look out for a gateway on your left, just beyond which a narrow bridleway heads into the wood signposted 'Bridleway Bakewell'.
DSF: 16.32 miles (27.26 km).

Q **Manners Wood:** Head down the hill into the wood for a short section of singletrack. Take care at the bottom as the track ends on a road.
DSF: 16.72 miles (26.91 km).

R **Castle Hill:** Turn left onto the road and roll down the hill, follow the road and turn left at the bottom and you're back at the car park.
TOTAL DISTANCE: 17.09 miles (27.50 km).

Route Nineteen

BAKEWELL – CHATSWORTH

Total Distance: 11.26 miles (18.12 km)

Off-road: 5.43 miles (8.74 km) (48%)

Time taken: 3½ hours

OS Map: Outdoor Leisure 24, *White Peak*

Start: Monsal Trail car park (GR SK222690)

Rail Access: not practical, but Padley Chapel if you're desperate.

Difficulty Ratings

Technical: ●●○○○

Fitness:　●●●○○

This ride takes you into, and through, the heart of the Peak District. It starts close to picturesque Bakewell, which is always good for a look round and a bacon butty. It also passes close to Chatsworth House which you can take a look at if you make a slight detour before you get through Edensor (pronounced 'Ensor'). It's well-signposted, and worth a visit if you haven't seen it before. The ride itself makes excellent use of local bridleways, though these can get muddy in the winter months, especially on the ascent through Rowsleymoor Wood and the surrounding plantations. And, of course, we've included some smashing downs, including the blast through the grass at New Piece Woods (try to stick to the bridleway) and one of the finest pieces of twisting singletrack we know of at Ballcross Farm/Manners Wood. All things considered, this ride makes for a fine day out.

The Route

A **Monsal Trail car park:** Turn right (SE) onto the Monsal Trail and cycle along the hardpack track until you reach the end of the trail (there's a sign that says 'End of Trail').
DISTANCE SO FAR (DSF): 0.83 miles (1.34 km).

B **Coombs Road:** Take the steep track that leads off down to the right to meet Coombs Road. Take a sharp left onto the Coombs Road which turns from tarmac to hardpack beyond Coombs Farm. Continue until you arrive at a fork in the road.
DSF: 2.04 miles (3.28 km).

C **Rowsleymoor Wood:** Turn left uphill (don't take the bridleway signposted for Chatsworth). After a brief climb, descend on hardpack through the trees, then on tarmac until you meet the main road.
DSF: 3.26 miles (5.25 km).

D **A6/Rowsley:** Turn right (W) onto the A6. Continue until you see the entrance to Haddon Park Farm on your right.
DSF: 5.19 miles (8.35 km).

E   **Haddon Park Farm Entrance:** Take the right turn and cycle uphill on tarmac. On the final straight up to Haddon Park Farm, look out for the bridleway off to the right signposted 'Public Bridleroad'.
DSF: 5.67 miles (9.12 km).

F   **'Public Bridleroad':** Take the bridleway on the right and head uphill on hardpack until you reach junction of paths.
DSF: 6.38 miles (10.27 km).

G   **Aaron Hole Plantation:** Take the left-hand path and cycle along on hardpack until you shortly reach another junction. (On the map, this is just a continuation of the bridleway).
DSF: 6.52 miles (10.49 km).

H   **Rowsleymoor Wood:** Take the track off left through a metal gate following the signpost for 'Bridlepath to Chatsworth'. Carry on uphill through the wood, following the track round to the left, ignoring the path off to the right. At a split in the trail, turn sharp right uphill, following the blue bridleway arrow. At the top, head through the gap in the stone wall and follow the track to the left into the trees. As you approach a wooden five-barred gate, the trail turns through 90 degrees to the right, again following the blue arrow. Drop down to the stile, keeping the stone wall on your left.
DSF: 7.30 miles (11.75 km).

I   **Calton Plantations:** Hop over stile, and follow the blue arrow that directs you across and down through the grassy field. At the bottom, follow the path round to the left, which brings you to another wooden five-barred gate. Head through the gate and turn immediately right, rolling down to meet a gate on your right, and a stone wall in front of you. Follow the path left uphill, across the field to meet a gate. Go through the gate and roll down to meet a second gate, which opens onto Chatsworth Estate.
DSF: 8.18 miles (13.16 km).

J   **New Piece Wood:** Through the gate and follow the

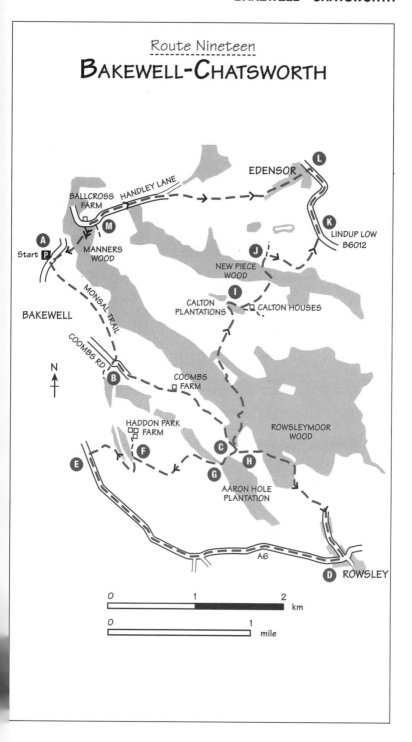

Route Nineteen
BAKEWELL-CHATSWORTH

EDENSOR

L

BALLCROSS FARM   HANDLEY LANE

K

LINDUP LOW
B6012

A

Start   P

M

MANNERS WOOD

J

NEW PIECE WOOD

I

CALTON PLANTATIONS

CALTON HOUSES

MONSAL TRAIL

BAKEWELL

COOMBS RD

B

COOMBS FARM

N

HADDON PARK FARM

F

E

ROWSLEYMOOR WOOD

C

H

G

AARON HOLE PLANTATION

D   ROWSLEY

A6

0   1   2   km

0   1   mile

grassy track that leads off to the right, following the contour of the hill. After a quarter of a mile, as the track approaches the edge of the wood, turn left to drop down the hill (the turn is marked by a marker post) following it down to meet the B6012.
DSF: 8.75 miles (14.08 km).

K   **B6012/Lindup Low:** Turn left onto the B6012 and cycle along it until you reach the village of Edensor on your left just before you leave Chatsworth Estate.
DSF: 9.25 miles (14.89 km).

Chatsworth House: make a detour from Edensor

L   **Edensor:** Turn left into Edensor and head straight through the village with the church on your left. Ride up the hill, the road gets steeper and the tarmac gives way to an unmettaled road until it meet Handley Lane. Turn left onto the road and continue the climb. Just as you crest the hill, look out for a gateway on your left. Just beyond this, heading into the wood, is a narrow bridleway signposted 'Bridleway Bakewell'.
DSF: 10.84 miles (17.44 km).

M   **Ballcross Farm/Manners Wood:** Head down the hill into the wood for a short section of singletrack. Take care at the bottom as the track ends on a road. Turn left onto the road, then almost immediately right, and you're back at the car park.
TOTAL DISTANCE: 11.26 miles (18.12 km).

Route Twenty
PARSLEY HAY

Total Distance: 13.08 miles (21.05 km)
Off-road: 12.76 miles (20.53 km) (98%)
Time taken: 2 hours
OS Map: Outdoor Leisure 24, *White Peak*
Start: Parsley Hay Visitor Centre (GR SK147638)
Rail Access: Not practical.

Difficulty Ratings
Technical: ●●○○○
Fitness: ●●○○○

This is a short loop through the gently rolling terrain of the
White Peak. It makes an ideal outing for those new to Mountain Biking, combining easy tracks and gradients with good
scenery and numerous picnic opportunities en-route. The
route makes extensive use of two old railway lines, the High
Peak Trail and the Tissington Trail and, as such, can be ex-
pected to be pretty flat and easy going in almost any
weather. The connecting section, on white roads, is a little
more challenging with a good fun downhill section thrown
in. Altogether, this ride is a pleasant day out for groups of
mixed ability and the well-equipped Visitor Centre at the
start can arrange bike hire for those who need it.

The Route

A **Parsley Hay Visitor Centre:** Turn left (S) out of the car park onto the High Peak Trail and cycle along the hardpack track for a short distance until it meets the Tissington Trail.
DISTANCE SO FAR (DSF): 0.27 miles (0.43 km).

B **Tissington Trail:** Take the right fork onto the Tissington Trail and continue in a roughly southerly direction. The track soon crosses the B5054. Continue until you are about to reach the second bridge; at this point take the track down to the left of the trail that takes you down to meet the road. If you want to check it's the correct bridge, look to your right (W) where you should be able to see the outskirts of Biggin.
DSF: 3.52 miles (5.66 km).

C **Over Hide Farm:** Turn left and cycle up the road until it meets a T-junction with the busy A515. Turn right onto the A515 and head straight across to meet the beginning of Cardlemere Lane, an untarmacked 'white' road, on the other side.
DSF: 3.84 miles (6.18 km).

D **A515/Cardlemere Lane:** Follow Cardlemere Lane (SE)

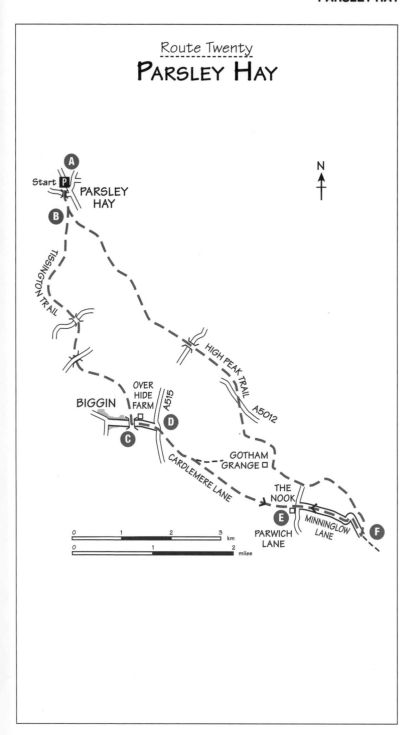

Route Twenty
PARSLEY HAY

N

A

Start
P

PARSLEY
HAY

B

TISSINGTON TRAIL

HIGH PEAK TRAIL

A5012

OVER
HIDE
FARM

A515

BIGGIN

D

C

GOTHAM
GRANGE

CARDLEMERE LANE

THE
NOOK

E

MINNINGLOW
LANE

F

PARWICH
LANE

0   1   2   3 km

0   1   2 miles

as it climbs gently upwards, for the most part between stone walls, and then enjoy the smooth downhill run that brings you out on Parwich Lane.
DSF: 5.89 miles (9.48 km).

E   **The Nook/Parwich Lane:** Go straight across Parwich Lane and begin the climb on the tarmacked Minninglow Lane, which soon deteriorates and gets steeper. Follow the track up through a gate at the top to meet the High Peak Trail.
DSF: 6.85 miles (11.02 km).

F   **High Peak Trail:** Turn left (NW) onto the High Peak Trail and stay on it until you reach Parsley Hay Visitor centre, you're a quick six miles from home. (If you're feeling peckish there's a rather nice food stop at Gotham Granges, just over one and a half miles along the trail). You'll be back at the car park in no time at all.
TOTAL DISTANCE: 13.08 miles (21.05 km).

THE LONG WEEKEND RIDE

We've designed this route with a long weekend in mind. Therefore, we've kept the first day's riding down to a little over eight miles to allow for all the travelling. It's also mainly on road, as it is a long hard climb out of Glossop. However, if you do live locally it should be easy to combine the first two days of riding. The ride is a sixty-mile loop which starts and finishes at Glossop Train Station, covering much of the Dark Peak in three days of superb riding. It is a ride that takes you across, and over, many places that are legendary amongst mountain bikers – Jacob's Ladder, Roych Clough, Chapel Gate Track, Cavedale and Mickleden Edge are all there. This is a weekend ride to savour, made up of the best that the Peak has to offer, it is a real off-road challenge.

Glossop – Hayfield – Edale – Glossop

We arrived in Glossop in the middle of a Friday afternoon. After a week's planning, packing and anticipation we were eager to get a start on our wicked, weekend route. Even on day one, we had some off-road fun over Matley Moor, and on the final descent into Hayfield over Middle Moor. By the time we got to our chosen B&B it was getting late, we were tired and felt we'd earned our rest.

On the morning of day two, we awoke feeling well up for it! We set off with drizzle at our backs, heading out for Mount Famine, and the white-knuckle descent into Roych Clough, which will test out any suspension. We greeted this like an old friend and really gave it some hammer. Over the years, we've left a lot of blood and skin here and this day was no exception because we're crazy boys. We do all our own stunts.

By the time we reached Castleton we were muddy, bloody and knackered, so we stopped in the Rose Café for a fantastic cream tea, before tackling the ascents up Goose Hill and up to Hollins Cross. Once at Hollins Cross we forced our tired legs to kick it one more time, down what is probably the smoothest, coolest, sheep-infested downhill that we know of, or that you could ask for, into Edale. We arrived at the YHA ready for a hot shower and a well-earned evening in the pub, chilling out with a few beers.

Day three arrived and we were eager to get on with what promised to be an awesome day's riding; it had even stopped raining. After a fine breakfast we set off with full stomachs, our water bottles filled with foul-tasting energy drink, ready for a long day in the saddle. A quick spin out of Edale and we were soon on the descent down to Jaggers Clough, which rocks, but which saw us fixing our first flat of the day. Pepped up by this 30 mph blast we splashed through the ford and made a brave start on the climb out of the other side. After a fair bit of pushing and a short granny-ring climb we were soon approaching the woods around Ladybower and looking forward to the infamous drop down Hagg Side where, predictably, we both ate dirt. Up the other side and there's yet another cool descent to the reservoir. After a brief spin on road, we were headed for the leg-sapping climb up Whinstone Lee Tor and down a real sharp drop to meet Ladybower Reservoir again. It was at this point that my brakes gave up. A word to the wise here, check your bike before you start off in the morning, because there are times when you'll wish that someone else was doing your stunts for you. From there, we blasted past the beautiful scenery of the reservoir and were soon up on Mickleden Edge, giving it as much as our legs would allow. Make sure you make the most of this, as it's the last piece of mean off-road you get this weekend. In just a couple of hours you'll be grinning manically at Glossop Station, or sitting in your car, applying plasters and discussing the coolest parts of this ride. Whichever way you get there or home, this is one sweet weekend.

Before You Go

Before starting off for the Peak District, make sure that you are prepared, that you know where you are staying, (i.e. book in advance) what the weather is going to be like and that you've got your waterproofs at the ready. We've prepared these handy lists to help you.

What to take

Firstly, you'll need something to carry your gear in. We'd avoid panniers and opt instead for a 25-30 litre rucksack, anything much bigger will only encourage you to take more than you need. We went for the *Berghaus Nitro*, which is a cycle-specific rucksack with plenty of space, a decent compression sys-  tem, and room for a standard one-litre hydration bladder. The *Nitro* is shaped to allow it to be worn at the same time as a helmet – make sure that your rucksack does the same. You need to look out for a bag with a relatively low pack height. We'd suggest that you take:

- Riding gear (helmet, shorts, gloves, waterproofs etc.)

- Bike repair kit (spare tubes, a pump, puncture repair kit, a multi-tool)

- Lightweight trousers, a spare shirt and a fleece, underwear.

- Wash Kit

- YHA card/money

- Compass, maps, torch, mobile phone

- Snickers/ bananas/ energy bars

- Water bottles (we're also advocates of bad-tasting energy drinks these days)

MOUNTAIN BIKING IN THE PEAK DISTRICT

Where to stay

All of the following places have said that they welcome
mountain bikers, and that they do have storage facilities for
bikes. However, this is not an exhaustive list of accommoda-
tion, and extra information is available from the Glossop
Tourist Information Centre. ☎ (01457) 855920.

Glossop

Avondale, 28 Woodhead Rd, Glossop. ☎ (01457) 853132.

Birds Nest Cottage, 40 Primrose Lane, Glossop. ☎(01457)
853478.

Bridge End, 1 Manor Park Rd, Glossop. ☎ (01457) 852559.

The George Hotel, Norfolk St, Glossop. ☎(01457) 855449.

Edale

Edale YHA ☎(01433) 670 302.

Hayfield

Beevers, 11 Highgate Rd, Hayfield. ☎(01663) 743288.

Bridge End, 7 Church St, Hayfield. ☎(01663) 747321.

George Hotel, Hayfield. ☎(01663) 743691.

Kinder Lodge, Hayfield. ☎(01663) 743613.

After a day's ride

Day One

GLOSSOP – HAYFIELD

Total Distance: 8.21 miles (13.21 km)
Off-road: 2.41 miles (3.88 km) (29%)
Time taken: 2-3 hours
OS Map: Outdoor Leisure 1, *Dark Peak*
Start: Glossop Station car park (GR SK035942)
Rail Access: you work it out.

Difficulty Ratings
Technical: ●●○○○
Fitness: ●●○○○

The Route

A   **Glossop Station car park:** Turn right out of the car
park and roll down the hill to the traffic lights. Turn
right onto to the A57 and cycle through Glossop's high
street and out of the town, past a couple of factories to
the second of two closely placed roundabouts. You
want the left exit signposted Simmondley.
DISTANCE SO FAR (DSF): 0.81 miles (1.30 km).

B   **Roundabout:** Turn left and ride up the hill. Stay with
the road as it climbs through Simmondley until you
reach Charlesworth. As you arrive at Charlesworth,
look out for a left turn leading steeply uphill signposted 'Chapel Brow leading to Monk's Road'.
DSF: 2.31 miles (3.72 km).

C   **Charlesworth:** Take the left turn up the hill. Continue
up this nasty climb for three-quarters of a mile after

which it heads back down. Look out for a right turn opposite Plainsteads Farm.
DSF: 4.06 miles (6.53 km).

D   **Plainsteads Farm:** Take the right turn and follow the
road around a sharp left turn. Head straight on to meet
a stile in the wall as the road turns sharply to the right.
DSF: 4.47 miles (7.19 km).

E   **Matley Moor:** Go over the stile and head across the
moor to meet a gap in the opposite wall. Through the
gap and head straight on through the gate opposite.
Take the track between two stone walls until it brings
you to Matley Moor Farm.
DSF: 5.11 miles (8.22 km).

F   **Matley Moor Farm:** Walk through the farmyard to
meet the farm road behind it. Head down the road to
meet the A624.
DSF: 5.86 miles (9.43 km).

G   **A624:** Turn left onto the A624 and cycle uphill until
you reach a bridleway on the right, opposite Carr
Meadow Farm.
DSF: 6.13 miles (9.87 km).

H   **Carr Meadow Farm:** Go through the gate and cycle
across the field and cross the bridge. Follow the track
upwards across the moor until you reach the white
'shooting cabins' at the top.
DSF: 6.67 miles (10.73 km).

I   **Shooting Cabins:** Take the track that leads off downwards to the right. Stay with it as moorland gives way to
grassland, finally taking you down across fields
(through several black 'kissing gates') to meet Bank
Street in Hayfield.
DSF: 7.90 miles (12.71 km).

J   **Bank Street:** Turn right onto Bank Street and follow it
downhill, take the first left, roll over the bridge and
you're in Hayfield centre.
TOTAL DISTANCE: 8.21 miles (13.21 km).

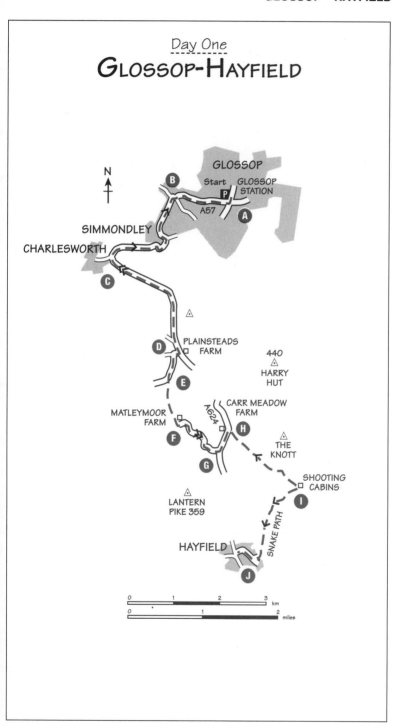

Day One
GLOSSOP-HAYFIELD

N

GLOSSOP

B Start GLOSSOP
STATION

A57 A

SIMMONDLEY

CHARLESWORTH

C

PLAINSTEADS
FARM

D

440
HARRY
HUT

E

MATLEYMOOR
FARM

CARR MEADOW
FARM

A624

F H

THE
KNOTT

G

SHOOTING
CABINS

LANTERN
PIKE 359

I

HAYFIELD

SNAKE PATH

J

0   1   2   3
km
0   .   1   2
miles

Day Two

HAYFIELD – EDALE

Total Distance: 22.31 miles (35.90 km)

Off-road: 15.04 miles (24.20 km) (67%)

Time taken: 4-5 hours

OS Maps: Outdoor Leisure 1, *Dark Peak* & Outdoor Leisure 24, *White Peak*

Start: Hayfield Church (GR SK037869)

Difficulty Ratings

Technical: ●●●●●

Fitness: ●●●●●

Mam Tor

The Route

A **Hayfield Church:** Head down the wide passage to the left side of the church to meet the A624. Cross the road to the Sett Valley Trail Visitor Centre opposite.
DISTANCE SO FAR (DSF): 0.06 miles (0.10 km).

B **Sett Valley Trail:** Head up the Sett Valley Trail for nearly a mile, until you see a factory building on the right. At this point, take the track up to the left that leads you to the A6015 in Birch Vale.
DSF: 0.96 miles (1.63 km).

C **Birch Vale:** Go straight across the A6015 to the road opposite that heads steeply uphill, signposted 'Public Bridleway & Lantern Pike'. Head up the road, which soon changes from tarmac to hardpack, at the top leave the road, which heads left, and join the bridleway that goes straight on through a wooden gate signposted 'Chinley via Chinley Churn'.
DSF: 1.52 miles (2.45 km).

D **Bridleway:** Head through the gate and onto bridleway and ride uphill across the moorland on the obvious track. Keep going until you reach a signposted junction at the top.
DSF: 2.34 miles (3.77 km).

E **Junction:** Take the left turn and follow the track down and then up to meet a gate. Over the brow of the hill, the track heads down, through the garden of Hill's Farm and then it's a steep down on hardpack through two gates and onto a final stretch of tarmac to meet the A624.
DSF: 3.35 miles (5.39 km).

F **A624:** Turn left on the A624 and almost immediately right onto a bridleway opposite next to the first house you see. Head uphill on the stony farm track taking the right turn, again uphill, when it reaches another bridleway. Continue until you reach a gate.
DSF: 3.93 miles (6.32 km).

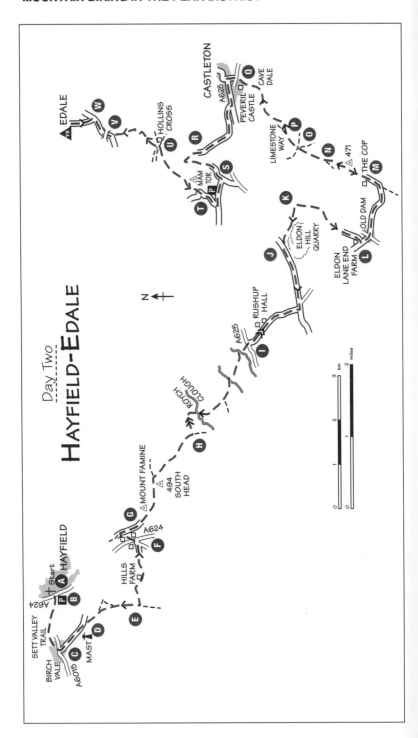

Day Two
HAYFIELD-EDALE

G **Mount Famine:** Go straight on and through the double gates. Follow the obvious track around to the left, then around to the right at South Head and downhill through a series of gates.
DSF: 5.55 miles (8.93 km).

H **Roych Clough:** Follow the main path through the left gate and take the rough track down to Roych Clough. Head through the gate at the bottom, cross the stream, and begin the climb up towards the A625. The track soon eases off and, after a nasty climb on steep broken ground, becomes an easy climb on hard-packed sandy ground ending at a gate by the A625.
DSF: 8.93 miles (14.37 km).

I **A625:** Through the gate and turn left onto the A625, taking the first right after fifty metres or so. Head down the road, which becomes 40 mph steep. At the bottom of the road turn left onto the B6061, continue uphill until you see Eldon Hill Quarry on the right, just past the quarry is the entrance to a wide hardpack bridleway heading uphill.
DSF: 10.76 miles (17.32 km).

J **Eldon Hill Quarry:** Head up the quarry road, past the quarry workings until the track starts to level out. Take the second of two metal gates on the right just past the Motocross track.
DSF: 11.44 miles (18.41 km).

K **Motocross Track:** Go through the gate and cycle across the field keeping to the left-hand wall, the track soon heads off downhill to meet a metal five-barred gate. Through the gate and onto tarmac past Eldon Lane End Farm to reach a T-junction with Old Dam Lane.
DSF: 12.63 miles (20.33 km).

L **Old Dam Lane:** Turn left onto the road and continue to the small roundabout. Take the left exit and head uphill past the houses until the road ends opposite a white farm house (The Cop).
DSF: 13.72 miles (22.08 km).

M **The Cop:** Head through the small gate and uphill following the blue arrow. Continue uphill between two
closely placed walls and go through the gate at the top.
Turn left and continue along the track keeping the wall
on your left until you reach a second gate. Go through
the gate and turn left, passing a small pond on the
right. Follow the wall down to meet a stile on the other
side of the field.
DSF: 14.42 miles (23.21 km).

N **Stile:** Turn right onto the track and follow it around to
the right along the side of the field until you reach a
crossroads at a gate.
DSF: 14.88 miles (23.95 km).

O **Limestone Way:** Go straight on passing through two
closely spaced gates. Ride down the smooth grass path
for 0.28 miles turning right at the first fork which brings
you to a small metal gate. Go through the gate into
Cavedale.
DSF: 15.16 miles (24.40 km).

P **Cavedale:** Once through the gate follow the path
down to the right. The track soon becomes rocky and
extremely technical, easing up toward the bottom.
DSF: 16.35 miles (26.31 km).

Q **Castleton:** Go through the gate at the bottom of
Cavedale and roll down the hill into the centre of
Castleton. Turn left at the church onto the A625 and
follow the road until it ends with a bus turning area at
the bottom of the old collapsed road, at the foot of
Goose Hill.
DSF: 17.69 miles (28.47 km).

R **Goosehill:** Simply follow the broken road up to the
top, through the gate and the car park, until you're at
the junction with the A625. Turn right.
DSF: 18.66 miles (30.03 km).

S **A625:** Follow the road for 0.42 miles until you reach
the right turn just after Mam Nick car park. Take the
right and uphill as the road starts to descend look out

for a bridleway entrance on the right marked by a bus stop sign.
DSF: 19.43 miles (31.27 km).

T   **Bridleway/Bus Stop:** Take the right turn off-road and follow the track along the contour of the hill, climbing gently before a short descent to meet Hollins Cross (Marked by a stone pillar).
DSF: 20.42 miles (32.86 km).

U   **Hollins Cross:** Take the left turn between stone gate-posts to head downhill, follow the track to meet a gate, go through it onto a farm road and follow it to meet a T-junction with the main road.
DSF: 21.40 miles (34.44 km).

V   **T-Junction:** Turn right onto the road and cycle until you see the YHA entrance on the left (it's signposted).
DSF: 21.86 miles (35.18 km).

W   **YHA Entrance:** Take the left and cycle up the hill until you reach the YHA itself.
TOTAL DISTANCE: 22.31 miles (35.90 km).

Ridge track near Hollins Cross

Day Three

EDALE – GLOSSOP

Total Distance: 38.00 miles (61.15 km)
Off-road: 31.01 miles (49.90 km) (81%)
Time taken: 5-6 hours
OS Map: Outdoor Leisure 1, *Dark Peak*
Start: Edale YHA (GR SK140866)

Difficulty Ratings
Technical: ●●●●○
Fitness:　●●●●●

The Route

A　**Edale YHA:** Head down the hill out of the YHA to meet the road at the bottom. Turn left onto the road and continue until you see a bridleway entrance heading uphill to the left. If you reach the entrance to Clough Farm, you've just missed the bridleway.
DISTANCE SO FAR (DSF): 0.76 miles (1.22 km).

B　**Clough Farm:** Go through the gate and begin the off-road climb through the trees. Out of the trees and the climb eases on a wide sandy track, after around three-quarters of a mile of climbing there's a fast descent around a hairpin bend to meet a gate beyond which a ford crosses the river.
DSF: 1.79 miles (2.88 km).

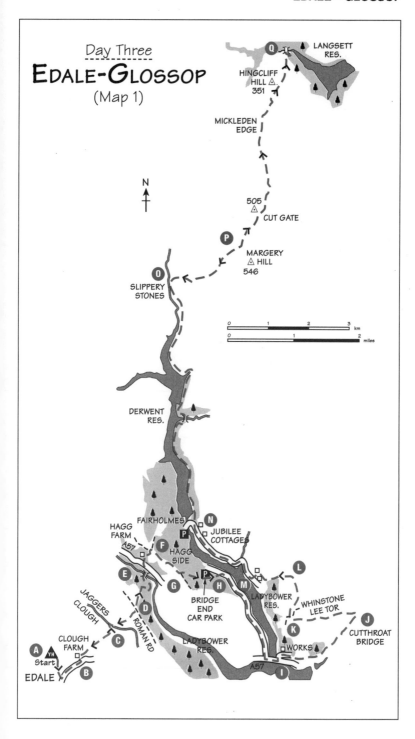

Day Three
EDALE-GLOSSOP
(Map 1)

LANGSETT
RES.

Q

HINGCLIFF
HILL △.
351

MICKLEDEN
EDGE

N

505
△
CUT GATE

P

MARGERY
△ HILL
546

O

SLIPPERY
STONES

0   1   2   3   km

0   1   2   miles

DERWENT
RES.

FAIRHOLMES

N

HAGG
FARM

JUBILEE
COTTAGES

P

F

HAGG
SIDE

A57

L

E

G

P

H

M

LADYBOWER
RES.

WHINSTONE
LEE TOR

J

BRIDGE
END
CAR PARK

JAGGERS
CLOUGH

D

K

CUTTHROAT
BRIDGE

CLOUGH
FARM

C

ROMAN RD

LADYBOWER
RES.

WORKS

A

YH
Start

B

A57

I

EDALE

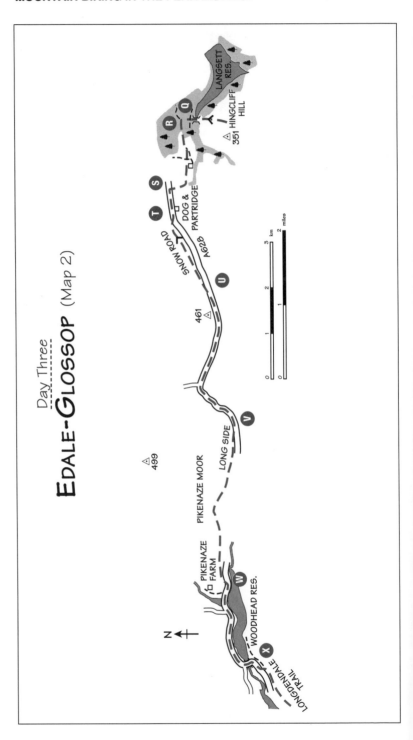

Day Three
EDALE-GLOSSOP (Map 2)

C   **Jaggers Clough:** Ford the river and head up the steep track on the other side. Continue along this well-marked track as it levels off until you reach a gate at the crossroads with the wide Roman Road.
DSF: 2.21 miles (3.56 km).

D   **Roman Road:** Go straight across the Roman Road following the signpost for 'Derwent via Hagg'. Drop down the rocky track to meet a gate, through that and onto the narrower technical (very rocky) track that twists its way down through the wood. Bear left at the bottom and the right over the bridge. Then it's a steep, but less technical, climb up to meet the A57.
DSF: 3.21 miles (5.17 km).

E   **A57:** Head straight across the A57 and climb up the tarmac road on the other side. Head up past Hagg Farm where the tarmac gives way to hardpack, head through the gate and up to meet a signposted crossroads.
DSF: 3.67 miles (5.91 km).

F   **Crossroads:** Take the right turn, signposted 'Public Bridleway Crookhill Farm'. Follow the obvious track along the side of the wood until you reach a gate and a left turn downhill.
DSF: 4.23 miles (6.81 km).

G   **Hagg Side:** Take the left, signposted 'Bridleway to Derwent Valley and Bridge End car park'. Follow the wide, downhill track through the trees, bearing left until you reach a gate onto the road at the bottom.
DSF: 4.89 miles (7.87 km).

H **Bridge End car park:** Through the gate and turn right onto the road and cycle along the side of the reservoir until you reach a T-junction with the A57. Turn left onto the A57 and cross over the reservoir. Immediately after you have crossed the bridge, look for a sharp left turn uphill, marked 'works entrance'.
DSF: 6.64 miles (10.69 km).

I **Works Entrance:** Head up the road which following it as it turns sharply to the right (don't go through the gate that heads straight on) past a small group of houses and through a wooden gate onto the bridleway. Follow this smooth track upwards for a short time and then down alongside a stone wall until you reach a T-junction with another track. Take the left turn uphill and follow the obvious track until the track forks just before the stream. You need the left fork.
DSF: 7.68 miles (12.36 km).

J **Cutthroat Bridge:** Head uphill and follow the sandy moorland track as it bears left, ignoring an early opportunity to head off to the right. Continue until you reach a five-way junction at the top.
DSF: 9.26 miles (14.90 km).

K **Whinstone Lee Tor:** At the top there are five paths to chose from. Two of these head to the right. Take the lower of these two right turns, following the blue bridleway arrow. Follow the path (which can get boggy) along the side of the stone wall as it follows the contour of the hill. After three-quarters of a mile, you will reach a gate in the wall that is signposted 'Derwent'.
DSF: 10.02 miles (16.13 km).

L **Gainfoot Clough:** Turn left through the gate and head across the field, aiming for the right-hand side of the wood. Stay with the well-defined bridleway until it takes you through a gate into a small courtyard with

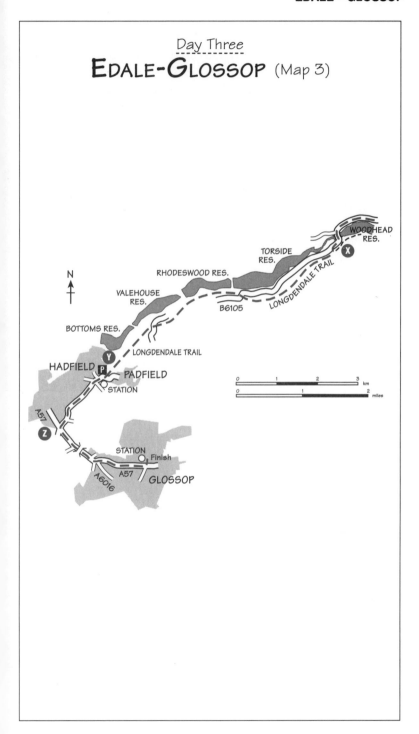

Day Three
EDALE-GLOSSOP (Map 3)

two old barns, head left through a narrow gate and onto a steep grassy descent that eventually meets a road at the side of the reservoir.
DSF: 10.84 miles (17.44 km).

M   **Ladybower Reservoir:** Turn right onto the road and follow it past several houses until, just past a turn-off that would lead you downhill past the dam you reach a bridleway heading off to the right (signposted with a blue arrow).
DSF: 11.96 miles (19.25 km).

N   **Jubilee Cottages:** Turn right onto the hardpack bridleway. Stay with it, ignoring all tracks that leave it to the left, until you reach a flatter area where a stone bridge crosses the river to your right and, slightly further on, your track crosses on a narrow wooden bridge.
DSF: 16.31 miles (26.25 km).

O   **Slippery Stones:** Following the sign for 'Langsett and Flouch Inn' cross the footbridge and head up the hill (NE). After an initially steep section, the track eases off to climb up across the moor, reaching a cairn at the top of Margery Hill.
DSF: 17.76 miles (28.58 km).

P   **Margery Hill:** Continue straight on. The track is fairly level for the first section, then drops following the course of a stream and is fairly rocky and technical. Eventually, the track smoothes out on Mickleden Edge, giving you a fast downhill. The final section twists around the side of a wood bringing you out at a stone bridge.
DSF: 21.16 miles (34.05 km).

Q **Bridge:** Cross the bridge and head up the steep climb on the other side. At the top head straight on into the trees until you meet a bridleway that leads off left sign-posted 'Flouch Inn & Hazelhead Station'.
DSF: 21.39 miles (34.42 km).

R **Crookland Wood:** Go left out of the wood until the track joins another path, take a right turn onto this path (which looks like straight on, on the OS map) and after a short climb turn right again onto Swinden Lane, signposted with a big blue arrow and 'Bordhill'. Go through the metal gate and follow the track between two stone walls until it ends. The bridleway heads off right up to meet the A628.
DSF: 22.56 miles (36.31 km).

S **A628:** Turn left (uphill) onto the A628 until you see a bridleway entrance on the right-hand side opposite the Dog and Partridge pub.
DSF: 22.88 miles (36.82 km).

T **Dog and Partridge:** Go through the gate and climb steadily up the farm track (Snow Road) until you meet the A628 once again.
DSF: 24.12 miles (38.82 km).

U **A628:** Turn right onto the road and head along it downhill until, just across a bridge, you see a sign-posted start to the Longdendale Trail on the right.
DSF: 26.07 miles (26.07 km).

V **Longdendale Trail:** Turn right onto the bridleway which heads west roughly parallel to the A628. Follow the track, a fairly wide semi-cobbled road that climbs gently up Longside, ending with a long off-road descent down Pikenaze Hill. At the bottom of the descent, head through the five-barred gate and roll down a short stretch of tarmac to meet the A628.
DSF: 28.67 miles (46.14 km).

W   **A628:** Turn right onto the A628, cross Woodhead bridge and ride along until you reach the left turn across Woodhead Reservoir, signposted 'Glossop – B6105'. Ride across the dam to rejoin the Longdendale trail.
DSF: 29.83 miles (48.01 km).

X   **Longdendale Trail:** Join the trail and turn right. Follow the trail until you reach its end at Padfield car park (there is one major road crossing about half way along the trail – the B6105).
DSF: 35.38 miles (56.94 km).

Y   **Longdendale Trail car park:** Turn right out of the car park and follow the road to the war memorial. Turn left past the station and go straight across at the top of the road onto Church Street keeping the church on your right. Continue straight on until you reach a T-junction with the A57.
DSF: 36.45 miles (58.66 km).

Z   **A57:** Turn left onto the A57 and follow it straight into Glossop town centre until you reach the turn off for the station on your left. Head left uphill and you've made it home.
TOTAL DISTANCE: 38.00 miles (61.15 km).

THE INFO SECTION

Peak District Weather News

Try Impact Weather Services ((01556 611117 or http://www.onlineweather.com) or any of the local information centres.

Information Centres

Bakewell	☎01629 813227
Buxton	☎01298 25106
Edale	☎01433 670207
Fairholmes (Derwent Valley)	☎01433 650953
Glossop	☎01457 855920
Macclesfield	☎01625 504114
Sheffield	☎01742 734671

Youth Hostels

The following is a list of the Youth Hostels in the Peak District and Sherwood Forest. It is advisable to book before arrival.

Bakewell	☎01629 812313
Bretton	☎0114 2884541
Buxton	☎01298 22287
Castleton	☎01433 620235
Crowden-in-Longdendale	☎01457 852135
Dimmingsdale	☎01538 702304
Edale	☎01433 670302
Elton	☎01629 650394
Eyam	☎01433 630335
Gradbach Mill	☎01260 227625
Hartington Hall	☎01298 84223
Hathersage	☎01433 650493
Ilam Hall	☎01335 350212
Langsett	☎0114 288541
Matlock	☎01629 582983
Meerbrook	☎01538 300148
Ravenstor	☎01298 871826
Sherwood Forest	☎01629 825850
Shining Cliff	☎01629 760827
Youlgreave	☎01629 636518

Bike Shops

This is our selection of the bike shops in and around the Peak District that we think are particularly good.

Mark Anthony Cycles 115 Spring Gardens, Buxton SK17 6BX. ☎ 01298 72114; fax 01298 73212

The Bike Factory Vernon House, Beech Road, Whaley Bridge SK23 7HP. ☎ 01663 735020

Stanley Fearn's Cycles 19 Bakewell Rd,Matlock DE4 3AU. ☎/fax 01629 582089

Harry Hall Cycles 19 Lever St, Manchester M1 1LW. ☎ 0161 236 5699; fax 0161 236 5699

J E James Cycles 347-361 Bramhall Lane, Sheffield S2 4RN. ☎ 0114 2550557; fax 0114 2550250. E-mail: info@jejames.demon.co.uk

KG Bikes 18 Norfolk Rd, Glossop, Derbyshire SK13 8BS. ☎ 01457 862427; fax 01457 869627

Cycle Hire

Ashbourne Cycle Hire ☎ 01335 343156

Carsington Cycle Hire and Water Sports Centre ☎ 01629 540478

Derwent ☎01433 651261

Middleton Top ☎01629 823204

Parsley Hay Cycle Centre, Buxton ☎01298 84493

Stanley Fearn's, Matlock ☎01629 582089

British Rail Booking Information

National Enquiries ☎ 0345 484950

County Council Offices (Rights of Way)

Derbyshire County Council, County Offices, Matlock, Derbyshire DE4 3AG. ☎ 01629 580000

Peak National Park, Aldern House, Baslow Rd, Bakewell, Derbyshire DE4 1AE ☎ 01629 816200

National & Local Cycling Clubs

Northern Area Mountain Bike Series ☎01282 430748
Cyclists Touring Club ☎01483 417217
Derbyshire MTBers ☎01246 204431 (Kevin Waddingham)
Derwent Valley All Terrain Club ☎ 01629 540395
KG Bikes, Glossop, run a club cycling on Thursday evenings
☎ 01457 862427
Matlock Bike Club ☎ 01629 734753 (Tony Holmes)

Trail Etiquette

For what they are worth, here are the 'Country' and 'Off
Road' codes. Use your common sense when you ride, be
nice and everything should go just fine.

THE COUNTRY CODE,
issued by the Countryside Commission

✔ Enjoy the countryside and respect its life and work.

✔ Guard against risk of fire.

✔ Fasten all gates.

✔ Keep your dogs under close control.

✔ Keep to public paths across farmland.

✔ Use gates and stiles to cross fences, hedges and walls.

✔ Leave livestock, crops and machinery alone.

✔ Take your litter home.

✔ Help keep all water clean.

✔ Protect wildlife, plants and trees.

✔ Take special care on country roads.

✔ Make no unnecessary noise.

THE OFF ROAD CODE, issued by the Mountain Bike Club.

⚴ Only ride where you know you have a legal right.

⚴ Always yield to horses and pedestrians.

⚴ Avoid animals and crops. In some circumstances this may not be possible, at which times contact should be kept to a minimum.

⚴ Take all litter with you.

⚴ Leave all gates as found.

⚴ Keep the noise down.

⚴ Don't get annoyed with anyone; it never solves any problems.

⚴ Always try to be self-sufficient, for you and your bike.

⚴ Never create a fire hazard.

Other Stuff To Do

Just in case you fancy doing something other than cycling while you're in the Peak District, here's a quick run down of what else is on offer.

Towns

Some of the towns in and around the Peak District particularly worth a visit include:

Ashford-in-the-Water – sheepwash bridge; well dressings

Bakewell – parish church; Saxon crosses; Bakewell tarts

Bradwell – Roman fort; Bagshawe Cavern; ice cream

Buxton – Pavillion; Opera House; Grin Low Country Park

Castleton – Peveril Castle; caverns; tea shops

Edale – Mecca for hikers and bikers

Eyam – plague village; lots of tea shops

Glossop – Roman fort of Melandra; Old Glossop for reminders of bygone times

Hayfield – stone-built village; Twenty Trees café

Hope – interesting old church; excellent Woodbine café

Miller's Dale – Monsal Trail; remains of old mill

New Mills – excellent Heritage Centre and Torrs industrial archaeological complex

Tideswell – home to the "Cathedral of The Peak"; well dressings

Whaley Bridge – busy canal wharf; near to Fernilee and Errwood reservoirs (with cycle routes)

Youlgreave – magnificent parish church; Youth Hostel; well dressings

Show Caves

Bagshawe Cavern 01433 814099

Blue John Cavern 01433 620638

Peak Cavern 01433 620285

Speedwell Cavern 01433 620512 (At 600ft this is the deepest cave open to the public in the UK but, apart from this and the fact that you see it from a boat, it hasn't that much to offer.

Treak Cliff Cavern 01433 620571(Probably the best of the lot, dripping with stalactites etc.)

Caving

For more information on caving courses and trips call the Pennine National Caving Club on 01831 44919.

Houses, Castles, etc . . .

Chatsworth House 01246 582204

Haddon Hall 01629 812855

Peveril Castle 01433 620613

Chestnut Centre 01298 814099 (otter and owl sanctuary)

ALSO OF INTEREST:

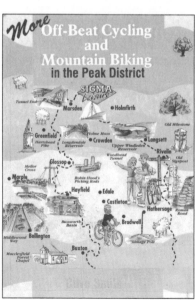

BY-WAY BIKING IN LANCASHIRE
Henry Tindell
From Morecambe Bay to Bolton and from Blackpool to Burnley, Henry Tindell reveals Lancashire's outstanding potential as a destination for mountain bikers. "A fine variety of off-road tracks lead you to a wealth of countryside and villages all within easy reach of the large northern towns and cities". BOLTON ADVERTISER £7.95

50 BEST CYCLE RIDES IN CHESHIRE
Graham Beech
"Every cyclist should be leaping into their saddles with this new book" THE CHESHIRE MAGAZINE. £7.95

OFF-BEAT CYCLING AND MOUNTAIN BIKING IN THE PEAK DISTRICT
Clive Smith
Cycle the tracks, bridleways and quiet lanes that cross the southern and central areas of the Peak District and link its picturesque villages - "Very useful" WEEKEND TELEGRAPH. £6.95

MOUNTAIN BIKING IN WEST WALES

Dave and Barbara Palmer

"Many people visit the area and bring their bikes but very few actually ride them ... they simply do not know where to go".

This observation prompted Dave & Barbara Palmer to write the first book of mountain bike routes in West Wales. *£6.95*

CYCLE EAST ANGLIA

Bob Shingleton

Cycling suits East Anglia - its fortuitous combination of quiet by-ways, timeless landscape, flat terrain and moderate climate is just made for the two-wheeled traveller. With rides in classic areas such as Cambridge and the Norfolk Broads, these 25 routes ranging from 10 to 35 miles help you get the best cycling out of the region - as well as providing notes on Sustrans' National Cycle Network *£6.95*

Our books are available from your local bookshop. In case of difficulty, or for our complete catalogue, contact: **Sigma Leisure, 1 South Oak Lane, Wilmslow, Cheshire SK9 6AR.**
Phone: 01625-531035.   Fax: 01625-536800.
E-mail: info@sigmapress.co.uk **Web site:** www.sigmapress.co.uk
MASTERCARD and VISA welcome.